Altar Server Manual

Serving in the Modern Roman Rite

Trainer Edition

ALTAR SERVER MANUAL

SERVING IN THE MODERN ROMAN RITE

TRAINER EDITION

PILGRIMAGE HOUSE PRESS
TACOMA, WASHINGTON
A.D. 2022

Altar Server Manual: Serving in the Modern Roman Rite Trainer Edition by Thom Ryng, Obl.S.B.

Pilgrimage House Press www.pilgrimagehousepress.com

ISBN 979-8-9867224-0-5

Illustrations on pages 17, 22, 36, 37, 90, 93, and 94 by Clara Fisher. "The Liturgical Calendar" on page 13 is modified from the work of Adam S. Keck as found in Wikimedia Commons; the original artwork was published under a Creative Commons Attribution-Share Alike 3.0 Unported license. Illustration on page 69 courtesy Corpus Christi Watershed, www.ccwatershed.org. Photographs on pages 37, 60, and 73 courtesy Melanie Wolf. Photograph on page 114 courtesy Francine Mastini. All other diagrams and photographs are by the author. Photographs were taken in cooperation with Our Lady of the Holy Rosary parish in Tacoma Washington, Rev. Francis Xavier Kikomeko, and the altar server families of Holy Rosary parish. All other illustrations in the public domain.

Ut In Omnibus Glorificetur Dei

Dedicated to the Altar Servers with whom I have served,

in memory of Dom Matthew Britt, O.S.B.,

and laid at the feet of Our Lady.

CONTENTS

FOR ALTAR SERVERS

GLOSSARY

APPENDICES

For Trainers

KEY TO SYMBOLS IN THE DIAGRAMS

Thurifer		C	Celebrant
Boat Bearer		Cc	Concelebrant
Cross Bearer		D	Deacon
S1 S2	Server 1, Server 2	D1 D2	Deacon 1, Deacon 2 (when more than one)
Book Bearer		B	Bishop
or Cn	Candle Bearer	Mb Cb	Miter Bearer / Crozier Bearer
Torchbearer		E	Extraordinary Minister of Holy Communion (EMHC)
MC	Master of Ceremonies	L	Lector

FOREWORD

THE MINISTRY OF ALTAR SERVERS is a normal part of the public worship of the Catholic Church. Since the beginning of Christianity, servers have found an honoured place and a defined role in the worthy celebration of the Divine Liturgy, whether according to the Roman Rite or the venerable Eastern Rites.

In the early Church, servers were called *acolytes*, from the Greek word for "followers". Yet going back even further to Jewish worship, we can see how their Christian role was derived from the *levites*, who assisted the priests in the rites and sacrifices in great Temple of Jerusalem. They also have a link with also the *attendants* who assist the rabbis in the synagogues[1].

However, as a bishop visiting many parishes, I have seen that this noble ministry is not always valued and esteemed. Some priests even dispense with servers altogether. In their churches, what happens at the altar becomes a "one man band". The celebrant may be accompanied by a lector, cantor, or ministers of Holy Communion, but he is not assisted by those "lay ministers" so clearly named and described in the ceremonial directives of the *General Instruction of the Roman Missal*[2].

The *General Instruction* sets out the need for servers and their basic roles. There should be at least one server to assist the priest[3]. Mass is not to be celebrated without a server, except for a just or reasonable cause[4]. One server may carry out all the various duties required[5], but the emphasis on specific roles makes it clear that this is not desirable.

There should be several servers at least, performing such roles as carrying the missal, cross, bread, wine, water and thurible[6]. To signify that they liturgical ministers, servers are to wear robes, either the alb or other vesture approved by the Conference of Bishops[7], such as the soutane and surplice.

The leading role in serving at the altar is the ministry of the *acolyte*, a layperson who has been instituted by the Bishop. Ideally, the head server or Master of Ceremonies is an officially instituted acolyte, trained to assist bishops, priests, and deacons in their sacramental and liturgical ministry.

However, even with the best intentions, serving may be trivialized, reduced to decorating the Mass with some quaint little children in costume. They have little to do so they do not know what they are meant to do. This may explain why they are still often incorrectly

---

1   *Cf.* Luke 4:20.
2   *General Instruction*, no. 100.
3   *General Instruction*, no. 115.
4   *General Instruction*, no. 254.
5   *General Instruction*, no. 110.
6   *General Instruction*, no. 100.
7   *General Instruction*, no. 339.

described as "altar girls" or "altar boys" and not "servers". While in practice most servers are young people, that is, older children and teenagers, serving is an *adult ministry*, one that has been granted to them according to local needs and customs. In parishes with a well-developed liturgy junior servers assist alongside adults.

Thom Ryng has given us a practical guide for serving Mass and other rites in the context of the parish. His guidelines are based, not only on respect for the liturgical laws of the Roman Rite, but on his own experience of supervising ceremonies in parishes in the United States. He takes into account the variations and local customs, but within the framework of liturgical law.

Therefore, Thom Ryng is concerned that servers should be properly trained, and here this manual is of great value. He provides practical strategies for training, planning and organising teams of servers, for example setting defined levels for serving based on age or experience. As a family man, he favors discipline, order and respect for a line of command!

Thom Ryng thus resolves another problem, that is unfortunately obvious in some places, when the servers do not know what they are meant to do or how to behave. Visitors coming to Mass are distracted even appalled by antics and confusion in the sanctuary. These young people were probably told "OK, you can serve if you want to" but then they were pushed out onto the altar and left to "learn on the job". We need to do better than that and, by insisting on planned training, Thom Ryng shows us concrete ways forward.

Most importantly, in this context of training, he understands serving at the altar in a *spiritual way*. We need to go deeper in training, beyond drilling soldiers to the personal *formation* of those Catholics who are involved in such a beautiful ministry.

As the Second Vatican Council taught, *all Christians are called to holiness*[8]. By bringing those called to serve more closely into the action of the "Sacred Mysteries", the experience of serving should draw them into a personal relationship with our Lord and only Savior, Jesus Christ. Prayer is the way this friendship and commitment develops, and cultivating a life of prayer underpins this manual. In this context, over many centuries, countless believers have also been able to discern what is their specific vocation in the Church.

I warmly commend this timely book. But it is not only meant to be read. It is meant to be used!

Most Rev. Peter J. Elliott

Auxiliary Bishop Emeritus, Melbourne
Titular Bishop of Manaccenser

---

8   *Cf. Lumen Gentium*, Dogmatic Constitution on the Church, 5.

PREFACE

The altar server occupies a privileged place in the liturgical celebration. He who serves at Mass, presents himself to a community. He experiences firsthand that Jesus Christ is present and active in every liturgical act. Jesus is present when the community comes together to pray and render praise to God. Jesus is present in the Word of sacred Scripture. Jesus is present above all in the Eucharist under the signs of bread and wine. He acts through the Priest who, in the person of Christ, celebrates the holy Mass and administers the sacraments. Therefore, in the liturgy, you are much more than simple "helpers of the parish Priest." Above all, you are servers of Jesus Christ, of the eternal High Priest.

— *Pope Saint John Paul II*

WHEN THE REVEREND JACOB MAURER RECONSTITUTED our altar server program at our parish of Holy Rosary in Tacoma in 2012, we found no good reference works in print on the training or even the duties of altar servers. The liturgical documents themselves are maddeningly vague on the duties, comportment, and training needs of altar servers[1]. Certainly, there are "guidebooks for altar servers" produced by several major Catholic publishers, but the information they contain is only of the most general sort. Of far more value were the books written on serving in the Extraordinary Form of the Mass. These books are typically precise, well organized, and often contain useful diagrams and illustrations. In particular, the two we initially found most useful were Father Carmody's *Learning to Serve* and Dom Matthew Britt's *How to Serve*[2]. While these books are a great foundation, they obviously do not address the movements and logistics of the modern, Ordinary Form of the Roman Rite. Adapting these books and using other sources, including of course the *General Instruction of the Roman Missal* and the *Roman Missal* itself, we cobbled together the first edition of this guide and began using it with our servers at Holy Rosary in 2014.

This current edition is much expanded and reorganized, taking advantage of hard-won experience, as well as the many sources that have become available in the passing years[3]. Chief among these sources is Bishop Elliott's *Ceremonies Explained for Servers*. This book, published in 2019 and available from Ignatius Press, is without a doubt the most complete and accurate guide available for serving in the Ordinary Form for altar servers and their

---

1   It has ever been thus. In 1934 Dom Matthew Britt observed "The rubrics provide a fair outline of the servers' duties; liturgical writers supply the details. The rubrics are often quite general, and at times none too clear. As a result they are not always interpreted in the same way. Custom, too, plays its part, even where there is no ambiguity in the law." (Britt, *How to Serve*, p. *x*)

2   Dom Matthew Britt O.S.B. was ordained in our parish church of Holy Rosary on June 24, 1901, back when it was a monastic church, and he also celebrated his first High Mass here a few weeks later on July 1, 1901. I like to think that we retained a bit of his spirit in the place.

3   See "Appendix 4: Additional Resources" on page 125.

trainers that is available in English. It is the ultimate guide on "what to do". Hopefully this book you hold in your hands will help fill in the "*how* to do it" part.

This book is intended primarily for the altar servers themselves. While those of a younger age may not go deeper into the details and symbols and meanings of the sacred liturgy, they will mature with both age and service in their ministry at the altar of the Lord, and these things will become of more importance to them. Many guides for youth talk down to them or presume that such things are "too complicated for kids". It has been our experience in this sacred ministry over the years that the more we ask of our servers, the more they give. When given a challenge, no matter how formidable, our servers have always risen to it.

We have tried to make this manual clearer using diagrams and photographs. As Father O'Connell wisely observed in his preface to *The Book of Ceremonies*, "the ministers... if they have once learned their ceremonies well, can in a very short time recall almost every movement they make during the Mass by studying the diagrams. Moreover, experience proves that the correct way to... genuflect, or to handle the thurible can be learned better from a drawing than from any amount of verbal instruction."[4] The sanctuary diagrams in this book represent an ideal church, arranged in the traditional manner. Of course, no building is ideal, but with an understanding of the principles and some diligence, they may be adapted easily enough to most circumstances.

I am indebted to the Reverend Jacob Maurer for his instigation and constant championing of this little volume, as well as his invaluable consultation during the process of revision; to the Most Reverend Peter J. Elliott who provided valuable insight and personally encouraged a wider publication of this book; to the Reverend Nicholas Wichert and the late Reverend Michael Wagner for their enthusiastic support of our altar server program and their words of encouragement; to those who have served at the altar at Holy Rosary church with dedication, reverence, and good humour; to those who supported our altar servers at Holy Rosary, especially Sister Hanh Kim Nguyen, L.H.C., Deacon Gary Rose, Mrs. Laurie Halte, and the ladies of the Holy Rosary Altar Society; to the members of the Holy Rosary Liturgy Commission for their enthusiasm, encouragement, and support; to those who reviewed the manuscript in whole or in part, including many of those mentioned above as well as my friends in the Society of Saint Odo of Cluny, the Reverend Joseph Levine, and the Reverend Joshua Nehnevaj; and finally and most importantly to my beloved bride Francine, without whom none of this would have been remotely possible. Although many hands have helped in the production of this book, any mistakes found herein are of course entirely mine.

May this little manual inspire Catholic youth and adults alike with a love for the altar and produce pious and faithful ministers of the sanctuary.

---

4   O'Connell, p. *x*.

APOLOGIA

On the Gestures and Bodily Postures of the Altar Servers

Liturgy is like a strong tree whose beauty is derived from the continuous renewal of its leaves, but whose strength comes from the old trunk, with solid roots in the ground.

— *Pope Saint Paul VI*

SERVING AT THE ALTAR IS much more than carrying the processional Cross before and after Mass. And yet, this attitude persists in many places. There are even those who believe that you can dispense with altar servers all together, that they are somehow superfluous or, even worse, a preconciliar throwback. Even a cursory reading of the *General Instruction of the Roman Missal* will refute these assertions. If anything, there is *more* asked of servers in the modern rite than there was in the past.

There are also those who will look at the instructions found in this book and dismiss them as hopelessly old fashioned or "not in keeping with the spirit of Vatican II". Once more, the *General Instruction* refutes these assertions. Again and again, it talks about the continuity of the rites[1]. Most explicitly, in section 42, we are instructed to pay attention to "the traditional practice of the Roman Rite" where it is not explicitly contradicted by the *General Instruction*. The passage in question specifically concerns gestures and bodily posture, and it's worth quoting the first paragraph in full.

> 42. The gestures and bodily posture of both the Priest, the Deacon, and the ministers, and also of the people, must be conducive to making the entire celebration resplendent with beauty and noble simplicity, to making clear the true and full meaning of its different parts, and to fostering the participation of all. Attention must therefore be paid to what is determined by this General Instruction and by the traditional practice of the Roman Rite and to what serves the common spiritual good of the People of God, rather than private inclination or arbitrary choice.

All the reverences and small gestures found in this book, then, rather than being fussy throwbacks, are to help show the resplendent beauty and noble simplicity of the rites. Through its long history, the Roman Rite has always displayed a measured solemnity which, while it may appear overfastidious to some in the modern age, is notable for its simple elegance when compared to the bombastic exuberance found in many of the Eastern Rites. There is nothing wrong with these grand and intricate gestures of the East,

---

1   Cf. *General Instruction*, nos. 1, 6*ff.*, 15, 41, 42, 59, 273, 301, 316, 318, 320, 326, 343, 346, 355, 357, 397*f.*

of course, but they are in their proper context in the Eastern Divine Liturgies. They are wholly inappropriate to the Roman Rite.

There are those who go to the opposite extreme and maintain a sort of liturgical minimalism, who claim that since the various bows and reverences that the servers may make are not specifically called for in the *Missal*, they must not be done. The fact is that the great majority of these gestures and postures are not called for in the older missals, either. They are not and never were explicitly demanded by the rubrics but instead belong to "the traditional practice of the Roman Rite".

So how do we know when it's appropriate to use these traditional gestures and movements? Section 42 gives us a hierarchy for determining this.

First, do what the *General Instruction* says. So, for example, in the older rites the servers knelt during the Penitential Act, but the *General Instruction* says that this be done standing[2]. So we stand.

Second, do what is traditional in the Roman Rite. For example, in the older rites the servers bow during the Penitential Act. Here, the *General Instruction* is silent. So we bow.

Finally, do what serves the common spiritual good rather than just making up something new. For example, while there is some flexibility about the details, nothing in the rubrics or the tradition permits the servers to adopt the *orans* position or to hold hands during the Lord's Prayer. So don't.

Of course, argument from the facts will only rarely change the opinion of those whose mind is already made up. Even so, Rome continually pleads for beauty and elegance in the Mass. Most recently, Pope Francis admonished ministers to "be vigilant in ensuring that every liturgy be celebrated with decorum and fidelity to the liturgical books"[3]. In fact, every Pope of the postconciliar period, as well as the Congregation for Divine Worship and the Discipline of the Sacraments[4], have regularly preached against liturgical minimalism in all its forms.

If we are to take seriously our ministry at the sacred liturgy–and how can we not?– surely we must pay attention to the teachings of those charged with its safekeeping.

2   *General Instruction*, no. 43.
3   Francis, Pope. Letter of the Holy father to the bishops of the whole world, that accompanies the apostolic Letter motu Proprio Data "Traditionis custodes". July 16, 2021. Accessed July 27, 2021. https://www.vatican.va/content/francesco/en/letters/2021/documents/20210716-lettera-vescovi-liturgia.html.
4   Now known as the *Dicastery* for Divine Worship and the Discipline of the Sacraments.

FOR ALTAR SERVERS

PRAYERS

Dear altar [servers], the closer you are to the altar, the more you will remember to speak with Jesus in daily prayer; the more you will be nourished by the Word and the Body of the Lord, the better able you will be to go out to others, bringing them the gift that you have received, giving in your turn, with enthusiasm, the joy you have received.

— Pope Francis

VESTING PRAYERS FOR ALTAR SERVERS

The vesting prayers should be recited quietly while vesting, either in Latin or in English. Begin with the Sign of the Cross and end with "Amen".

Alb
Dealba me, Domine, et munda cor meum;
ut, in sanguine Agni dealbatus,
gaudiis perfruare sempiternis.

Make me clean, O Lord, and cleanse my heart;
that being made white in the Blood of the Lamb
I may deserve an eternal reward.

Cincture
Præcinge me, Domine, cingulo puritatis,
et exstingue in lumbis meis humorem libidinis;
ut maneat in me virtus continentia et castitatis.

Gird me, O Lord, with the cincture of purity,
and quench in my heart the fire of concupiscence,
that the virtue of continence and chastity may abide in me.

Cassock
Dominus, pars hereditatis meæ et calicis mei,
tu es qui restitues hereditatem meam.

O Lord, the portion of my inheritance and my chalice,
You are He who will restore my inheritance.

Surplice
Indue me, Domine, novum hominem, qui secundum Deum creatus est
in iustitia et sanctitate veritatis.

Invest me, O Lord, as a new man, who was created by God
in justice and the holiness of truth.

PRAYER OF THE SERVERS BEFORE LEAVING THE SACRISTY

Just before Mass begins, the Priest (or M.C.) and Servers bow to the Crucifix.

℣. Procedámus in páce.

[Let us proceed in peace.]

℟. In nómine Chrísti. Amen.

[In the name of Christ. Amen.]

or

℣. Procedámus in páce. ℟. In nómine Chrísti. Amen.

Prayer before Mass–Psalm 43 (42) with Antiphon

℣. In the name ✠ of the Father, and of the Son, and of the Holy Spirit.

℞. Amen.

℣. I will go to the Altar of God.

℞. Unto God, Who giveth joy to my youth.

℣. Judge me, O God, and distinguish my cause from the nation that is not holy: *
deliver me from the unjust and deceitful man.

℞. For Thou, O God, art my strength: *
why hast Thou cast me off ?
and why do I go sorrowful whilst the enemy afflicteth me?

℣. Send forth Thy light and Thy truth: *
they have led me and brought me unto Thy holy hill,
and into Thy tabernacles.

℞. And I will go in unto the Altar of God: *
unto God, Who giveth joy to my youth.

℣. I will praise Thee upon the harp, O God, my God: *
why art thou sad, O my soul? and why dost thou disquiet me?

℞. Hope thou in God, for I will yet praise Him: *
Who is the salvation of my countenance, and my God.

℣. Glory be to the Father, and to the Son, *
and to the Holy Spirit.

℞. As it was in the beginning, is now, and ever shall be, *
world without end. Amen.

℣. I will go to the Altar of God.

℞. Unto God, Who giveth joy to my youth.

℣. Our help ✠ is in the Name of the Lord.

℞. Who made heaven and earth.

PRAYER AFTER MASS—BLESSING OF THE SERVERS

Upon approaching the Cross after Mass.

PRIEST: Prosit.

[May it (the Mass) be for your benefit.]

SERVER(S):   Pro omnibus et singulis.

["For all and for each", pronounced: pro OM-nee-boos et SING-oo-lees.]

The altar servers will also implore a blessing saying,

SERVER(S) OR M.C.:

Jube Domine Benedicere.

["May the Lord bless us", pronounced: you-bay DOE-me-nay ben-ay-DEE-cher-ay]

PRIEST: Benedictio Dei Omnipotentis ✠ Patris, et Filiis, et Spiritus Sanctis
Descendat super vos et maneat semper. Amen.

[May the blessing of Almighty God ✠ the Father, and the Son, and the Holy Spirit
Descend on you and remain with you always. Amen.]

An Introduction to the Sacred Liturgy

The Church stands and falls with the Liturgy. When the adoration of the divine Trinity declines, when the faith no longer appears in its fullness on the Liturgy of the Church, when man's words, his thoughts, his intentions are suffocating him, then faith will have lost the place where it is expressed and where it dwells. For that reason, the true celebration of the Sacred Liturgy is the centre of any renewal of the Church whatever.

— *Pope Benedict XVI*

THE CATHOLIC CHURCH IS THE SAME all over the world[1]. No matter where you go, Catholics believe the same things and celebrate the same Holy Mass and Sacraments. All are united with the Holy Father in Rome. It's important to remember that in different parts of the world, Catholics offer the same Holy Mass in many different ways. It all depends on what *rite* you belong to. In the Catholic Church there are many different rites. Each rite has its own language, and each rite has its own official way of praying, which we call *the sacred liturgy*. Most Catholics, including us, belong to the Roman Rite, which itself has several different forms[2].

Many other Catholics, however, belong to what we call *Eastern Rites*. They use Greek or some other language. Each rite has its own official prayer books written in its own language. For the Roman Rite, our official prayer books are written in Latin and translated into other languages, like English or Spanish or Vietnamese.

All these official prayer books have text printed in two colors–black and red. The prayers are printed in black, but the rules that tell us what to do are printed in red letters. In Latin, the word for these red letters is *rubrica*. In English we call them *rubrics*.

Rubrics are the rules for the Mass. Together with the guidebook to the Mass called the *General Instruction of the Roman Missal* and the traditions and customs of the Roman Rite, the rubrics tell us when to stand, sit, kneel, turn around, bow, and a lot of other things. Part of your job as an altar server will be to learn the rubrics and customs for serving Mass and other liturgies. You don't just make it up as you go along or wander randomly around the altar–you must serve according to the rubrics and customs.

---

1. These opening paragraphs are adapted and updated from Carmody, pp. 17–18.
2. Principally the *Ordinary Form of the Roman Rite*, with which this book is concerned. Other forms include the *Extraordinary Form* (which is exclusively celebrated in Latin and sometimes called the "traditional Latin Mass" or other names) and the *Ordinariate Form* (which is celebrated in English by former Anglican communities which are now in union with the Pope).

THE HOLY SACRIFICE OF THE MASS

If we only knew how God regards this Sacrifice, we would risk our lives to be present at a single Mass.

— *Saint Padre Pio (1887–1968)*

If you think Mass is boring, it might be because you don't know what you're experiencing! Many of us think of Church as that place you have to go on Sunday as a duty to God. That's not wrong, but it's not the whole story. God created us, and just as we have duties to our own parents and families, we have duties to God. We owe God reverence, and we have to thank Him for creating us and creating the world. But there is so much more than this!

God wants us to be free from sin, sorrow, and death, and the liturgy is the way that those things are overcome. Just like a father wants his child to grow up happy and healthy, God the Father through the Son wants us to grow up to be holy and perfect, just as He is perfect.

The Second Vatican Council summed it up this way: "The liturgy… is rightly seen as an exercise of the Priestly office of Jesus Christ."[1] What does that mean? Two thousand years ago, if you were living in Galilee, you could have met Jesus in the flesh. He was walking around, teaching the people, healing the sick, washing away sin, redeeming the fallen. And today He is *still* doing those things–and He is doing them through the sacraments[2]. The liturgy is nothing less than the saving work of Jesus Christ continuing in the world to the present day. *The liturgy is the ongoing work of redemption.* It is how Christ through physical signs and symbols glorifies the Father in the unity of the Holy Spirit and sanctifies humankind.

But as amazing as that is, that's not all! When we participate in the liturgy on earth, we are also participating in the *Heavenly liturgy*. The Heavenly liturgy is celebrated by the angels, the saints, and the "great multitude which no man could number, from every nation, from all tribes and peoples and tongues"[3]. In the sacraments, heaven truly comes to earth. When we sing *sanctus, sanctus, sanctus* we're singing the song that Saint John heard the heavenly choirs singing[4]. Whenever we celebrate the sacred liturgy, we touch eternity.

When the Priest raises up the precious body and precious blood, that is Christ at the last supper prefiguring His own sacrifice–instituting the Eucharist for His disciples while He still walks the earth. And at the same time, during the sacrifice of the Mass, that is Christ's sacrifice at Calvary. For just the briefest moment, time and space don't matter–and we are there, kneeling at the foot of the Cross with the Blessed Virgin Mary and Saint John. We are witnesses and participants with all the heavenly hosts and with all the faithful past, present, and future. We transcend the mere bounds of time and space to kiss eternity.

You can't get more exciting than that!

---

1. *Sacrosanctum Concilium*, no. 7.
2. *Cf.* St. Leo the Great, *Sermo* 74, §2.
3. Revelation 7:9.
4. Revelation 4:8.

An Introduction To The Sacred Liturgy

THE ORDER OF MASS

The Mass is primarily divided into two halves. We start with the *Liturgy of the Word*, where we listen attentively to the Word of God found in scripture. Then we move on to the *Liturgy of the Eucharist*, where the Priest *in persona Christi Capitis*[1] –in the very person of Christ, the Head of the Body of the Church–re-presents Christ's own sacrifice on the Cross.

The various parts of the Mass are listed below. You will see that some of these parts only happen on Solemnities, or on specific holy days of the year. There is a difference between an ordinary Thursday and the great feast of Holy Thursday! For more information on this, see "Progressive Solemnity" on page 11.

Prior to Mass

Before Mass, it is the custom in many places for the Priest and altar servers to pray together. In some places, they pray the traditional psalm and antiphon (see "Prayer before Mass–Psalm 43 (42) with Antiphon" on page 5).

Introductory Rites

- Entrance Procession / Entrance Antiphon (*Introit*)
- Reverencing of the altar and greeting the people.
- Penitential Act (by custom the *Confiteor*, except during Easter, when many parishes use the Sprinkling Rite on weekends.)
- *Kyrie eleison* (Lord have Mercy)
- *Gloria in Excelsis* (Glory to God; not sung in Advent, Lent, or most daily Masses)
- Collect (Opening Prayer)

The Liturgy of the Word

- Proclamation of the First Reading
- Responsorial Psalm
- Proclamation of the Second Reading (on Sundays and Solemnities)
- Sequence (only on Easter Sunday, Pentecost Day, Corpus Christi, and the Memorial of Our Lady of Sorrows[2])
- Acclamation before the Gospel (*Alleluia*, or tract in Lent), and the Gospel procession
- Proclamation of the Gospel
- Homily
- Following the Homily, additional rites may take place, including Baptisms. See "Sacraments and Ceremonies" on page 10.
- Profession of Faith (Normally the Nicene Creed; on Sundays and Solemnities)
- Universal Prayer (i.e. the Prayers of the Faithful)

---

1. *Catechism of the Catholic Church*, no. 875.
2. These last two are, strictly speaking, optional.

The Liturgy of the Eucharist

- Offertory (Presentation of the gifts and preparation of the altar, accompanied by the Offertory Chant. The Priest incenses the gifts on Sundays and Solemnities.)
- *Lavabo* (The Priest washes his hands.)
- Prayer over the Offerings

Eucharistic Prayer (the Canon of the Mass)

- Preface
- *Sanctus* (Holy, Holy, Holy)
- First half of Eucharistic Prayer, including the Consecration
- *Mysterium Fidei* (the Mystery of Faith)
- Second half of Eucharistic Prayer, ending with the Doxology (Through Him, with Him, and in Him...)

Communion Rite

- The Lord's Prayer (*Pater Noster* / Our Father)
- Rite of Peace (Sign of peace is optional; some parishes omit it during Lent.)
- Fractioning Rite (*Agnus Dei* / Lamb of God)
- Communion (accompanied by the Communion Antiphon)
- Purification of the vessels by the Priest and/or Deacon[1]
- Prayer After Communion

Concluding Rite

- Announcements (Optional)
- Blessing and Dismissal. Mass ends with the dismissal: everything after this is by custom rather than by rubrics.
- Prayer to Saint Michael (in many parishes)
- Recessional
- Blessing of Servers (see "Prayer after Mass–Blessing of the Servers" on page 6)

SACRAMENTS AND CEREMONIES

Different ceremonies for the celebration of the sacraments and other important events in the life of the Church are sometimes celebrated within the Mass. These include Baptisms, Confirmations, Weddings, and Funerals. If you are asked to serve in any of these, pay careful attention to the instructions of the M.C. and Priest. A summary of each can be found in "Appendix 1: Serving at Other Celebrations and Rituals" on page 101.

Guidelines for serving at Vespers may be found in "Appendix 3: Vespers" on page 121.

---

1. This may be done after Mass instead.

Progressive Solemnity

The basic idea of "progressive Solemnity" is that on "higher" feasts, we celebrate the Mass with the full ceremonial of the Roman Rite, whereas on ferias–ordinary daily Masses–a more restrained form of ceremonial is observed. Not every day is Christmas! Note that on some days, the use of additional altar servers may be required for some specific part of the ceremonial, a Holy Water Bearer, for example. The extreme example is the Easter Vigil, where between 11 and 20 altar servers can be usefully employed in a large parish.

Here is one suggestion for observing progressive solemnity, including the number of candles present on the altar and altar servers required.

Greater Solemnities

Candles...... 6[1]
Servers .... Cross Bearer, Book Bearer, Server 1, Server 2, Thurifer, Boat Bearer, M.C.
Torches 6

Solemnities

Including Sundays and Vigil Masses.

Candles...... 6[1]
Servers .... Cross Bearer, Book Bearer, Server 1, Server 2, Thurifer
Optional .... Boat Bearer, M.C.
Torches ...... 2, 4, or 6

Feasts

Including Ash Wednesday and All Souls' Day.

Candles...... 4
Servers .... Cross Bearer, Book Bearer, Server 1, Server 2, Thurifer
Optional .... Boat Bearer, M.C.
Torches ...... optional

Memorials / Ferias

Candles...... 2
Servers .... One or two altar servers suffice for daily Mass
Torches ...... no

Note: In addition to the above, the Paschal Candle is to be lit during all liturgies of the Easter Season, as well as during all Baptisms and funerals throughout the year.

---

1. Whenever the Diocesan Bishop celebrates, seven candles are lit. *Cf. General Instruction* no. 117.

LITURGICAL COLORS

The vestments of the Priest and Deacon have different colors for different seasons and feasts of the year. Each of these colors has one or more symbolic meanings, which remind us of the mysteries being celebrated.

In the modern Roman Rite, the following colors are used[1]:

Color	Meaning	When Used
White	Light, innocence, purity, triumph, glory	• Easter Season, • Christmas Season; • Solemnity of the Most Holy Trinity, • celebrations of the Lord (other than of His Passion), • celebrations of the Blessed Virgin Mary, • celebrations of the Holy Angels, • celebrations of the Saints who were not Martyrs, • Feast of the Conversion of Saint Paul (January 25), • Feast of the Chair of Saint Peter (February 22), • Solemnity of the Nativity of Saint John the Baptist (June 24), • Solemnity of All Saints (November 1), • Feast of Saint John the Evangelist (December 27); • Sacraments of Baptism, Matrimony, and Holy Orders; • Benediction of the Blessed Sacrament; • May be worn in Offices and Masses for the Dead, including All Souls'. • Wear gold cincture when the Priest wears white, except for funerals.
Red	The Passion of the Lord, the Holy Spirit, blood, fire, God's Love, martyrdom	• Palm Sunday of the Lord's Passion, • Friday of Holy Week (Good Friday), • Pentecost Sunday, • celebrations of the Lord's Passion, • Feast days of Apostles and Evangelists (except Saint John), • Celebrations of Martyr Saints, • Sacrament of Confirmation.
Green	Hope, growth, eternal life	• Ordinary Time.
Violet	Penitence, sorrow for sin, waiting for the Lord	• Season of Advent, • Season of Lent, • Holy Saturday (except the Easter Vigil), • Sacraments of Reconciliation and Anointing of the Sick, • May be worn in Offices and Masses for the Dead, including All Souls'. • Wear violet cincture for funerals.

---

1. *General Instruction*, nos. 345–347.

Color	Meaning	When Used
Rose	Joy of anticipation for Christmas and Easter	• Gaudete Sunday (Third Sunday of Advent), • Lætare Sunday (Fourth Sunday in Lent). • Violet may be substituted on these days if rose is not available. • Wear rose cincture. If none are available, wear violet.
Black	Mourning, sorrow	• All Souls' Day. • May be worn in Offices and Masses for the Dead, including All Souls'. • Wear violet cincture.
Gold	Majesty, joy, celebration	• Gold may substitute for any other color, particularly on more solemn days and seasons such as Christmas and Easter. • Wear gold cincture when the Priest wears gold, except for funerals.

On more solemn days, more precious sacred vestments may be used, even if they are not the color of the day.

The Priest(s) and Deacon(s) should wear matching vestments, and the chalice veil and burse should likewise match. Except where otherwise indicated on the chart, female servers (who are not apprentices) also wear a cincture of a matching color.

THE LITURGICAL CALENDAR

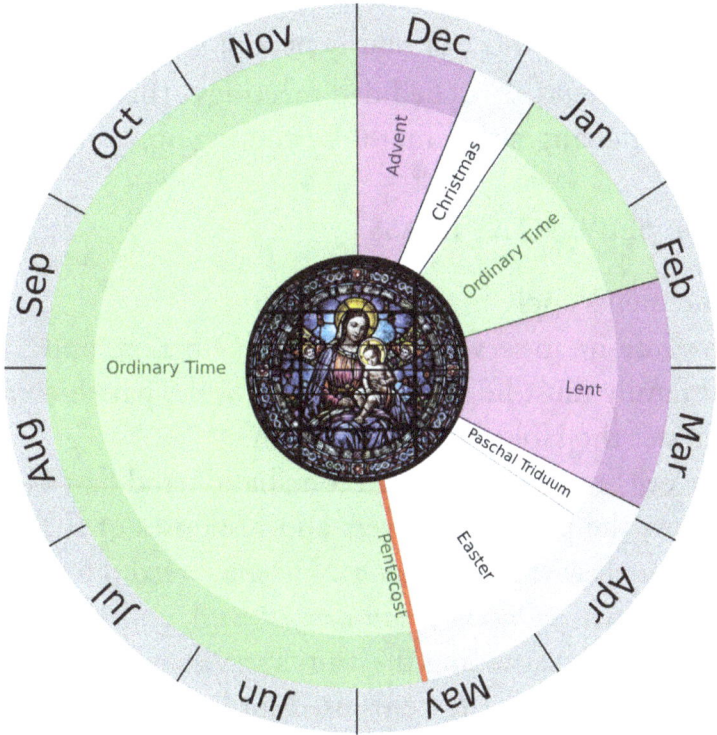

The seasons of the Liturgical Calendar that are based on the date of Easter (Lent and Easter Seasons) move around the calendar from year to year, depending on the date of Easter in any given year. Easter is on the first Sunday after the first full moon after the spring equinox, so it can be as early as mid-March or as late as the end of April.

GENERAL INFORMATION FOR SERVERS

Thank you for serving at the Lord's altar and for making of this service a real school of learning the faith, and charity toward your neighbor. Thank you also for having begun to respond to the Lord, like the prophet Isaiah, "Here I am. Send me" (Isaiah 6:8).

— Pope Francis

YOU WILL BE SERVING AT THE altar of the Lord! Any Catholic can serve, so long as they have received their First Holy Communion[1]. There is no mandated maximum age. The Church has a centuries-long history of both adults and youth as servers. You are welcome to stay in the Lord's service for as long as you wish to remain. As you serve, however, you should keep in mind that there are guidelines and rules for altar servers, as there are for any important job, whether within the Church or elsewhere.

ATTENDANCE

Every altar server must attend every Mass for which they are scheduled. If you cannot be present, you must arrange for a replacement. You are on duty from the moment you enter the sacristy before the start of Mass until you finish cleanup after the end of Mass. During the Mass, your duty station is in the sanctuary, and you may not leave the sanctuary except as directed by a Priest, Deacon, M.C., or bodily necessity.

Altar servers should also attend any scheduled meetings. This is where you find out about any special celebrations or changes that might be coming up.

REQUIREMENTS FOR SERVING AT MASS

The following requirements apply to all candidates:
1. You must have a desire to serve at the Altar of Our Lord and Savior, Jesus Christ.
2. You and your family must be active members of the parish community and believe in the teachings of the Holy Catholic Church.
3. You must have celebrated your first Reconciliation and first Holy Communion.
4. You should know the principal prayers and responses of the Mass: the *Gloria*, the Lord's Prayer (Our Father/*Pater Noster*), Nicene Creed, Holy, Holy, Holy (*Sanctus*), Lord, I am not worthy (*Domine, non sum dignus*), and Lamb of God (*Agnus Dei*). There is nothing more distracting than altar servers who do not know these prayers.
5. You should be familiar with the items used for liturgical purposes.
6. You must demonstrate the ability to make use (both tactfully and ceremonially) of the "tools of the trade" such as matches, candle lighters, books, and candles.

---

1. "Guidelines for Altar Servers", no. 3.

Appropriate Dress

Dress in your Sunday best. Your knees, shoulders, and everything in between must be covered. All footwear should look neat, presentable, and dressy.

Young men are to wear:
- A plain shirt in a solid color, preferably white or black.
- Long pants, preferably black but at least a dark color.
- Black dress shoes with matching dark socks

Young women are to wear:
- Plain white blouse or a plain shirt in a solid color
- Long skirt or pants, preferably black.
- Black flats with nylons or matching dark socks. No heels please!

Do NOT wear:
- Shorts or jeans.
- Athletic shoes, sandals, or cowboy boots.

Jewelry

All Jewelry must be taken off and placed in a pocket before Mass begins. This includes rings, earrings, bracelets (including the rubber or string ones), and watches. An exception may be made for a wedding ring worn by an adult altar server.

If worn, necklaces and scapulars must be covered by your vestments.

Hair

Hair should be neat and clean and out of your eyes. If you have long hair, you must wear your hair pulled back in a bun or ponytail. Hair must be a natural color.

Appropriate Demeanor

In and out of the sanctuary, the altar server represents the Church to some degree, and therefore their conduct and demeanor should be respectful and reverent. Servers must realize that their behavior and conduct set an example to others both inside and outside of the church.

An altar server must want to serve at the Altar of God. Their decision to serve, with parental support, is always the main motivating factor. A reluctant or disinterested altar server is a distraction during the Mass.

An altar server must not chew gum or have a cell phone on during Mass.

VESTURE

To signify your role as ministers in the sacred liturgy, altar servers are to wear sacred vestments. The vestment common to all ordained and instituted ministers of any rank is the alb, tied with a cincture. Cassock and surplice may substitute for this[1].

Altar servers should always pray the appropriate vesting prayers while vesting[2].

When choosing a vestment, altar servers must be careful that their alb or cassock is not too long for them. It should extend to about two or three inches above the floor, just brushing the top of the shoes. The sleeves should reach to the hand. It should also not be too short. If a choice must be made between *slightly* too long and *slightly* too short, always choose slightly too short. Even experienced altar servers can be tripped up by long vestments.

The albs and surplices worn by altar servers at any given Mass should be uniform or at least in harmony with each other.

Albs and surplices with a moderate amount of lace should be restricted to the M.C. and the most senior (Master) Servers, and extensive lace decoration is more properly reserved to clergy[3]. It is customary that the use of lace should be avoided entirely on days where the liturgical colour is violet or black[4].

Alb and Cincture

The alb is a long, white garment that reaches from the neck to the heels, and it is normally tied by a cincture. The alb is a symbol of baptism, reminiscent of the baptismal garment. If the alb does not sufficiently cover the collar, an amice should be worn as well[5].

The cincture is a cord fastened about the waist to hold the alb in place. It represents purity.

Cassock and Surplice

The cassock (or soutane) is a long, black garment that reaches from the neck to the heels. It is worn by some altar servers and clergy. It traditionally has 33 buttons (representing Christ's earthly years), though the simpler versions available for altar servers will usually have fewer.

The surplice is a white garment that goes over the cassock. It was originally a shortened form of the alb. Like the alb, it is a symbol of baptism. The end of the surplice should fall between the waist and the knees.

---

1. *General Instruction* nos. 336, 339. Given its long historical association with the minor orders and the clergy, it seems advisable to restrict the surplice to male altar servers.
2. *Compendium on the Eucharist*, pp. 318–319. Although this instruction is focused on the vesting prayers of the Priest, there is no reason to suppose that the vesting prayers of the altar servers (or the Deacon!) should be ignored. See "Vesting Prayers for Altar Servers" on page 3.
3. Fortescue, p. 54.
4. Lent, Advent, funerals, etc.
5. *General Instruction* nos. 119, 336.

SURPLICE

ALB

CASSOCK

CINCTURE

SUMMARY

Servers strive to mature in the following:
- Be vested at least fifteen (15) minutes before the start of Mass.
- Be silent and respectful in the sacristy.
- Follow the dress code. Face and hands are to be clean.
- Be attentive and reverent in the sanctuary.
- Memorize and clearly enunciate the Mass responses. Sing when required!
- Maintain correct posture and proper positioning.

COMMON CEREMONIAL ACTIONS

Servers… exercise a genuine liturgical function. They ought, therefore, to discharge their office with the sincere piety and decorum demanded by so exalted a ministry and rightly expected of them by God's people. They must have a deep sense of the spirit of the liturgy and be trained to perform their functions in a correct and orderly manner.

(Sacrosanctum Concilium–the Constitution on the Sacred Liturgy, 29)

RUBRICS ARE RULES THAT PRESCRIBE WHAT must be done during a liturgical action. Rubrics make it possible for a group of people to act as one or as a single unit. In compiling the rubrics in this manual, special attention has been paid to the *General Instruction of the Roman Missal* (or *General Instruction* for short), the *Ceremonial of Bishops*, and "the traditional practice of the Roman Rite"[1]. This section of "Common Ceremonial Actions" are all things you should learn to do as an Apprentice Server. Additional actions are covered in the next chapter, "Advanced Ceremonial Actions" on page 33.

GENERAL RULES

No matter how complicated a ceremony becomes, it is still built on simple rules. If you know these simple rules by heart, it will help you greatly in any ceremony at all.

1. All actions are performed slowly and smoothly and as noiselessly as possible.
2. One action is always fully completed before a second action is begun. Rising, sitting, and kneeling are three separate movements.
3. Always move forward. Avoid walking sideways or backwards (but see "Sitting" on page 20). Never pop up or down. Never slide into a kneeling position.
4. Eyes are normally lowered. Never stare into the congregation or gaze absently around the sanctuary. When seated or kneeling, look towards the place where the action is happening: the ambo or the altar. When a Lector is proclaiming the scriptures, you should be looking at the Lector.
5. Partners must perform actions together. When turning around, they turn toward each other. Groups of altar servers must be very careful to perform their actions smoothly and together.
6. Unless holding something or otherwise being used, hands are always properly folded. In serving, when one hand is occupied, the other hand is always over your heart. When seated, your hands are extended flat on top of your thighs.
7. Pay attention to the M.C., or if there is no M.C., the Celebrating Priest, in case he needs your assistance.

---

1. *Cf. General Instruction* no. 42.

STANDING, SITTING, AND KNEELING

As an altar server, you have three primary positions during the Mass when you are not performing a specific duty. These are standing, sitting, and kneeling. In any of these positions, maintain a straight formal posture. Rising, sitting, and kneeling are three different movements. Some altar servers seem to think that the three are all one, and they slide up and slide down. *Never do this.* Rising, sitting, and kneeling all must be done separately.

Standing

The altar server has a definite position, which is called their *stance*. You can always tell a well-trained altar server by their stance. Here is the stance, your position of attention:

> **Head**–keep your head straight, with eyes lowered.
>
> **Body**–hold your body straight with shoulders back. Do not lean against the furniture or against the walls.
>
> **Feet**–keep your feet together, except when in motion.
>
> **Knees**–keep your knees flexible. Locking your knees for a long period can cause fainting!
>
> **Joined Hands**–except when sitting, if the hands are not in use, they are to be palm-to-palm, hands pointing diagonally towards Heaven, with the right thumb over the left thumb in the form of a cross. The fingers are held together firmly[1].
>
> Be careful not to have the hands too high or too low. Don't let them droop and don't put them near your mouth. Always keep the fingers fully extended and joined; never fold them one over the other; never interlock them. A good altar server always keeps their hands in the correct position.

When standing, never slouch. Remain still with your body facing straight ahead. At the proclamation of the Gospel, turn your whole body towards the *Book of the Gospels*.

---

1. *Ceremonial of Bishops* no. 107.

Sitting

Sit down on your chair carefully and gracefully. Once you are seated, sit tall and do not slouch. Place both feet firmly on the floor. Place the palms of each hand flat on each leg with fingers together and extended.

When wearing a surplice, it should rest on the lap, not stretched out. When wearing an alb, it should likewise rest and not be stretched.

Keep your eyes on the action at the altar or the ambo if appropriate. Otherwise, keep your eyes firmly fastened straight ahead of you, slightly down. Nobody in the congregation wants to see an altar server staring at them from the sanctuary.

Kneeling

When you kneel, your body should be upright and your hands in "joined hands" position.

Sometimes, your alb or cassock can get tangled up in your feet when you go to stand up. Be sure to remove your alb or cassock from your shoes before you stand. When you kneel, the best way to keep your vestments from tripping you when you stand back up is to grab and pull them forward away from you as you kneel down. Try to kneel down with the entire bottom hem of the vestment several inches in front of both feet. When you stand, pull the garment out again, if necessary, to prevent putting either foot on it. A little practice is all that is needed to learn this and for it to become automatic.

WALKING

Walk slowly and evenly. Don't wobble. Remember: head up, eyes down, shoulders back, hands in place, and slow, even steps. There's no hurry.

Going up and down steps can be a problem. Watch where you are going, especially if you are carrying something. Never walk and bow at the same time. Always come to a full stop before you bow or genuflect.

Walking in Formation

When altar servers walk together, they normally walk in pairs shoulder to shoulder. Servers rarely walk by themselves. Other formations include the "Cross and Candle" formation, the "Triangle" formation, and the "Box" Formation.

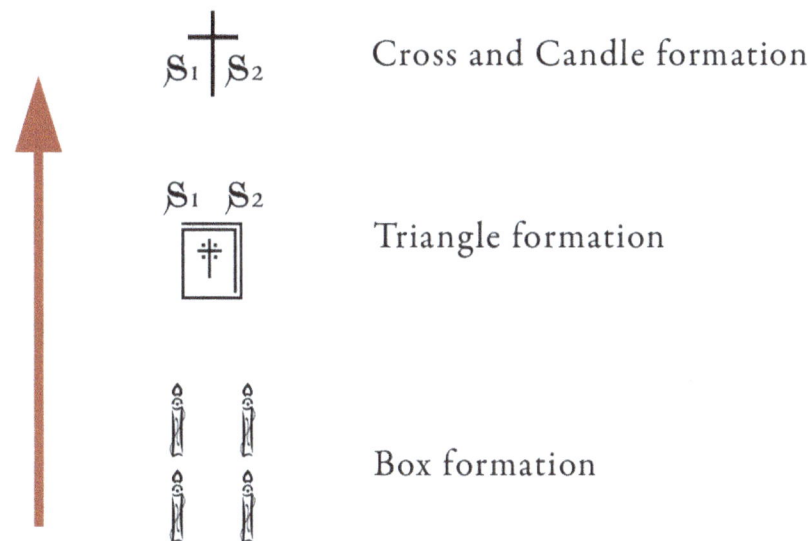

Cross and Candle formation

Triangle formation

Box formation

The Cross and Candle formation consists of the Cross Bearer flanked by Server 1 and Server 2, normally with candles. When this formation comes to a narrow space, such as a doorway, the Cross Bearer always walks ahead, while the other altar servers pair up behind the Cross. When they come out of the narrow space, they resume their original formation.

The Triangle formation consists of three altar servers. It is most often seen in the Mass during the arranging of the altar, when Server 1 and Server 2 walk as a pair with the Book Bearer behind them[1], forming a triangle.

The Box formation is found most often in processions, especially the four-candle Gospel procession. It consists of two pairs of altar servers who may change partners when they change direction.

---

1. During a Mass celebrated *ad Orientem*, that is, on the high altar or a side altar, the triangle is reversed, with the Book Bearer leading the pair of Server 1 and Server 2.

Turns

There are three kinds of turns: the *Sweep*, the *Turn in place*, and the *Back-sweep*.

Sweep: In a sweep, a formation of altar servers turn to the left or right around a common axis, like a door turns around a hinge. This means that the "inside" altar server is moving at a slower speed than the "outside" altar server. This takes careful practice, particularly when one of the altar servers is very much taller or shorter than the other.

The Sweep

Turn in place: If you both have to turn around together to move in the opposite direction, for example when two altar servers turn away after offering wine and water to the Priest or Deacon, turn in towards one another.

Back-sweep: This is normally only done when taking your place in a pew, where the altar server closest to the pew is the hinge, and the "outside" altar server steps backwards to finish by standing at their seat. This is almost the only time an altar server should move backwards.

Processions

When walking in procession remember that you are on parade. Your main duty is to look dignified and prayerful and to add beauty to the ceremony. Be certain to walk with head erect but eyes down, with hands properly joined. Always walk evenly with your own partner and keep about three or four pews behind the person ahead of you. Don't bunch up!

THE SIGN OF THE CROSS

All things we do at church are in the Name of the Father, and of the Son, and of the Holy Spirit. We use the holy water upon entering the church to remind us of our baptismal promises, which were done in His Name. We begin and end the celebration of the Mass in worship and praise of Him. All blessings we receive, or pray for, are granted by Him.

How: From the "joined hands" position, place your left hand over your heart. The sign of the cross is made with the right hand.

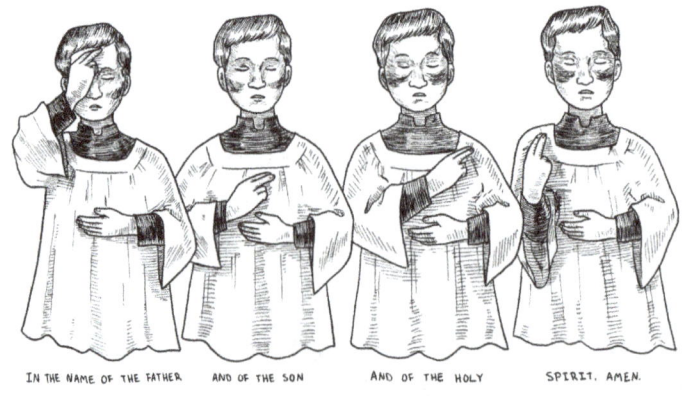

IN THE NAME OF THE FATHER   AND OF THE SON   AND OF THE HOLY   SPIRIT. AMEN.

When:

- At the beginning of Mass, when the Priest begins "In the name of the Father, and of the Son, and of the Holy Spirit"[1]. Remember to bow as well for the Holy Trinity.
- When the Priest begins the absolution following the *Confiteor* ("May almighty God have mercy on us..."), come out of the bow and make the Sign of the Cross[2].
- During the *Gloria*, unless you are holding something, make the Sign of the Cross at the end, during the words "in the glory of God the Father" (*in gloria Dei Patris*)[3].
- *Sanctus*: unless you are holding something, make the Sign of the Cross during the words "Blessed is he who comes in the name of the Lord" (*Benedictus qui venint in nomine Domini*)[4].

The Small Sign of the Cross

How: From "joined hands" position, place your left hand over your heart. The fleshy side of the right-hand thumb makes a small cross on the forehead, over the lips, and just above the left hand, praying silently: "O Lord bless my mind (*forehead*), my mouth (*lips*), and my heart (*chest*) that I may worthily hear your Holy Gospel."

When: After the Priest announces the Gospel reading and we say, "Glory to You, O Lord." As we are about to receive the Good News, we pray that the Word of God will be on our mind, on our lips, and in our heart.

GENUFLECTING

"A genuflection... signifies adoration, and therefore it is reserved for the Most Blessed Sacrament, as well as for the Holy Cross from the solemn adoration during the liturgical celebration on Good Friday until the beginning of the Easter Vigil."[5] There are two kinds of genuflections—the single and the double. The single is made with one knee and the double with two knees, plus a shoulder bow. In all genuflections, go straight down and straight up. Don't speed through it. Don't pop up and down. Don't place your hands on your knee, and above all don't wobble.

---

1. *General Instruction* no. 124.
2. O'Connell, p. 163.
3. O'Connell, p. 163.
4. O'Connell, p. 165.
5. *General Instruction* no. 274. Note that this abrogates the former custom of also genuflecting to a first class relic of the Passion (which may still be done outside of Mass as a personal devotion). Although there is no current legislation on the matter, in *Compendio di Liturgia Pratica*, Rev. Trimeloni recommends a simple bow to relics exposed for veneration.

Single Genuflection

The single genuflection is by far the more common of the two. Genuflect toward the tabernacle where the Blessed Sacrament is reserved and do so each time you pass in front of it (except while you are serving during Mass).

When genuflecting, keep these points in mind:

1. Keep the body and head erect.
2. Keep the hands in place.
3. Slowly bend the right knee to the floor. The knee should reach a position opposite the left heel.
4. After the knee touches the floor, slowly, but immediately rise and take your stance.
5. If you were walking somewhere, turn and continue in the direction you were heading.

The rules for when to genuflect and when to bow are different depending on whether it is during Mass or not. For the purposes of these rules, Mass begins when the Priest enters the sanctuary, and it ends when he leaves.

Single and Double Genuflection

When to Genuflect: Before or After Mass

In places where the tabernacle is located in the sanctuary (i.e. not in a separate Eucharistic chapel of reservation), be sure to face the tabernacle and genuflect with the Priest when you arrive at the sanctuary at the beginning of Mass and when leaving at the end[1]. When you are carrying things like Crosses or candles, bow your head instead[2].

The presence of the Eucharist in the tabernacle is signified by the lit sanctuary light. When it is not lit, the tabernacle is empty. This normally happens only on Good Friday and Holy Saturday. During those times, do not genuflect; instead bow to the altar as you do during Mass.

Do not genuflect during Mass; instead bow to the altar where the sacrifice takes place. A profound bow is made to the altar of sacrifice by all who pass before the altar[3].

When to Genuflect: During Mass

There are two exceptions to the rule of not genuflecting during Mass:
1. On the Solemnities of the Annunciation and of the Nativity of the Lord (Christmas), during the Creed all genuflect at *et incarnatus est,* etc. "and by the Holy Spirit was incarnate of the Virgin Mary and became man"[4].
2. When the Priest or Deacon genuflects in obtaining or reserving the Eucharist in the tabernacle, all altar servers should simultaneously genuflect with him.

Double Genuflection

Whenever Jesus is present on the altar in a monstrance during Eucharistic adoration, a genuflection is required when entering or exiting the church or sanctuary or passing in front of the monstrance. In places where the custom has been maintained, this should be a double genuflection.
1. Keep the body and head erect.
2. Keep the hands in place.
3. Slowly bend the right knee to the floor. The knee should reach a position opposite the left heel.
4. After the knee touches the floor, lower your left knee so that you are in a kneeling position.
5. Shoulder bow.
6. Slowly rise and take your stance.
7. Turn and continue in the direction you were heading.

---

1. When you are serving at another church, always respect the custom of the place, remembering especially that "if the Blessed Sacrament is set a long way back from the main altar, in what is really a separate area, it may be the local custom to bow to the altar, rather than genuflecting to the distant tabernacle." (Elliott, *Ceremonies Explained for Servers*, no. 181)
2. *General Instruction* no. 274 paragraph 5. This abrogates the ancient custom that the Cross Bearer never bows or genuflects (*cf.* Fortescue p. 44).
3. *Ceremonial of Bishops* no. 72; *General Instruction* no. 274.
4. *General Instruction* no. 137.

Practical Advice for Genuflecting

When you genuflect in your alb or cassock, it is best to move the left foot forward and keep the right foot stationary as you kneel. Always genuflect on the right knee. When you rise, again keep the right foot stationary and draw back the left.

If you do not have room to move your left foot forward, then you must move your right back. You must be careful in getting up to keep your vestment out of the way of that right foot! This may require you to pull the vestment forward with your hand as you kneel down and as you raise your knee.

BOWING

In the Roman Rite, we bow to the altar, the crucifix, and the Priest and other sacred ministers. We do not genuflect or kneel to any person or thing except God[1]. The *General Instruction* notes that there are "two kinds of bow: a bow of the head and a bow of the body"[2]. It then goes on to differentiate between two different kinds of bows of the body[3], which we will here call the *profound bow* and the *shoulder bow*.

Simple, Shoulder, and Profound Bows

There were once three different degrees of head bow[4], but these are no longer observed.

---

1. By way of exception, genuflect to the Cross when it is presented for veneration on Good Friday.
2. *General Instruction* no. 275.
3. *General Instruction* no. 275 b.
4. Indicating *dulia*, *hyperdulia*, and *latria* respectively. O'Connell, p 35.

Head Bow

The head bow (sometimes called the "simple bow"[1]) is made by lowering your chin to your throat and holding it there for a moment. Only the head is bowed. The shoulders are not moved. Be careful not to jerk your head! This should be a smooth movement. The majority of bows made by altar servers during the Mass are of this type.

You should bow your head[2]:
- Any time you hear "Father, Son, and Holy Spirit" mentioned together (but also see "Profound Bow" on page 28)[3].
- Any time you hear the Holy Name "Jesus"[4].
- Any time you hear the name of the Blessed Virgin Mary. Do not bow if a different Mary is mentioned.
- During Mass, when you hear the name of the Saint in whose honor the Mass is being celebrated. Again, do not bow if another saint with the same name is mentioned. Do not bow if the name is mentioned as part of the title of the reading or Gospel[5].
- If you would normally be required to genuflect to the tabernacle or perform a profound bow to the altar, but you are carrying something (such as a Cross or candle), you should perform a simple bow instead[6].
- When ministering to a sacred minister (see below).

Ministering to a Sacred Minister

Bow your head before and after any presentation or immediate action in serving a sacred minister. This includes:
- During the preparation of the altar if handing sacred vessels to the Deacon or M.C.
- When receiving the gifts[7] at the Offertory.
- When presenting the cruets during the Offertory.
- During the lavabo[8].
- Before receiving communion[9].
- During the ablutions and clearing of the altar.

---

1. Or *caput inclinat* (Fortescue, p. 45).
2. The first four instances in this list are mentioned in *General Instruction* no. 275 a.
3. Many monastic and formerly monastic churches retain the custom of making a profound bow at the mention of the Blessed Trinity.
4. This custom dates back to Apostolic times, though it was only written into law by the Second Council of Lyons, convened by Pope Gregory X in 1274 (Constitution 25).
5. E.g. "A reading from the Letter of Saint Paul to the Ephesians", or "from the Holy Gospel according to John".
6. *General Instruction* no. 274 paragraph 5.
7. If the Priest or Deacon performs a shoulder bow instead, you should mimic his action.
8. Including occasions outside of the Liturgy of the Eucharist, e.g. following the imposition of ashes on Ash Wednesday or during the *Mandatum* (washing of the feet) on Holy Thursday.
9. *General Instruction* no. 160 paragraph 3. If you are kneeling, however, there is no need to also bow.

Body Bow

Shoulder Bow

Sometimes called a moderate bow or (in the *General Instruction*) a slight bow[1]. Both the head and shoulders are bowed. Do not bow too deeply–but remember to bow slowly.

- During the Act of Penitence maintain a shoulder bow throughout[2]. When the Priest begins the absolution ("May almighty God have mercy on us…"), come out of the bow as you make the Sign of the Cross.
- If you are kneeling when the Priest genuflects during the Eucharistic prayer[3].
- When the Priest take his communion[4].
- During Benediction[5], while kneeling with the Blessed Sacrament exposed:
  - before you stand to help the Priest or Deacon put incense in the thurible,
  - before and after incensing the Blessed Sacrament, and
  - during the *Tantum Ergo* at the words *veneremur cernui*.

Profound Bow

Sometimes called a deep bow[6]. Bow deeply at the waist. Don't speed through this; the movement should be smooth, not jerky.

- If you are serving in a church where there is no tabernacle in the sanctuary, bow to the altar with the other ministers upon entering the sanctuary before Mass[7] and upon leaving after Mass[8].
- *During Mass only*, bow each time you pass in front of the Altar *where the sacrifice of the Mass is celebrated*[9]. Do this instead of genuflecting (or bowing) to the tabernacle.
- During the Creed, make a profound bow during the words "and by the Holy Spirit was incarnate of the Virgin Mary and became man" (*et incarnatus est*, etc.)[10].
- If you are standing when the Priest genuflects after the consecration[11].
- When the Priest or Deacon says "bow down for the blessing"[12].

---

1. Fortescue calls this a medium bow or *inclinatus* (Fortescue, p. 45).
2. Fortescue, p. 99, with the understanding, however, that in the Ordinary Form of the Roman Rite, the altar server stands rather than kneels during the *Confiteor* (*General Instruction* no. 43).
3. O'Connell, pp. 160–161.
4. Fortescue, p. 102.
5. Fortescue, p. 298–299.
6. Or a low bow or *profunda inclinatio* (Fortescue, p. 44).
7. *General Instruction* no. 122.
8. *General Instruction* no. 169.
9. *General Instruction* no. 274.
10. *General Instruction* no. 137; "but on the Solemnities of the Annunciation and of the Nativity of the Lord, all genuflect."
11. *General Instruction* no. 43.
12. *General Instruction* no. 185. In some communities it is the custom to perform a simple bow instead. This is no doubt held over from the abrogated 1970 translation, "[b]ow your heads and pray for God's blessing".

- Before and after incensation, a profound bow is made to the person or object that is incensed[1].
- Many monastic and formerly monastic churches retain the custom of making a profound bow at the mention of the Blessed Trinity. If this is the case at your parish, do this any time you hear "Father, Son, and Holy Spirit" mentioned together.
- At a pontifical Mass[2], a profound bow is made to the Bishop:
  - whenever approaching or assisting him,
  - when leaving him after assisting him, and
  - when passing in front of him[3].

If several bishops are present in the sanctuary, only bow to the one presiding[4].

Never make a profound bow while kneeling. If there is some circumstance that would seem to require it, make a shoulder bow instead.

STRIKING THE CHEST

This ancient gesture is done as a symbol of recognition that we are sinners.

How: From the "joined hands" position, place your left hand over your heart. Cup your right hand into a loose fist and tap your chest slightly above the left hand.

When:

- ***Confiteor:*** three times while saying "through my fault, through my fault, through my most grievous fault" (*mea culpa, mea culpa, mea maxima culpa*)[5].
- ***Agnus Dei:*** unless you are holding something, strike your breast each time you say "have mercy on us" (*miserere nobis*) and "grant us peace" (*dona nobis pacem*)[6].
- ***Lord, I am not worthy:*** unless you are holding something, strike your breast during the words "not worthy that you should enter under my roof" (*non sum dignus ut intres sub tectum meum*)[7].

---

1. *General Instruction* no. 277, *Ceremonial of Bishops* no. 91.
2. That is, any Mass with a Bishop.
3. *Ceremonial of Bishops* no. 76.
4. *Ceremonial of Bishops* no. 78.
5. *Roman Missal,* p. 515.
6. Fortescue, p. 101.
7. Britt, p. 10.

How to Carry Objects

From time to time, you will be called upon to carry the candles, torches, the processional Cross, or aspersory. Here are a few tips for each one.

Note that when you are carrying a sacred object, hand gestures are never required. When one hand is in use, the free hand is placed flat over the heart.

Candles

The candle carried by the altar server is the symbol of Christ–the Light of the World. Therefore, the candle should be held high, firm, and straight up and down. Be careful not to tip it or hold it crooked. If you do, wax may drop on the floor or on your vestments.

In holding the candlestick, place your outside hand (the farthest from your partner) on the candlestick, just below the central node. Place the inside hand on the base of the candlestick, grasping the bottom[1]. When you carry a candle, you do not genuflect, but bow your head instead.

Torches

In solemn ceremonies and processions, there may be torchbearers. You must be careful not to wobble your torch. All the torches should be held at the same height and perfectly straight. Before you bow, place the torch quietly and firmly on the floor first, so you don't accidentally bang it on the floor when you bow.

When walking *inside* the church, always hold the torch in your outside hand and away from your body (otherwise, this will cause the torch to lean). This hand should also be about six to eight inches below the candle socket in order to hold it steady. Your unoccupied hand is placed flat over your heart.

When walking *outside*, carry the torch in both hands, with your outside hand on top.

Processional Cross

The processional Cross is the sign of our salvation and should be held aloft with dignity. Place both hands on the staff of the Cross. Place the right hand high on the staff and the left hand lower on the staff. Keep the figure of our Lord (the "corpus") facing forward. If you hold the Cross out from you a little bit, you will not kick it or bump it as you walk.

Carry the Cross slowly and with great dignity.

---

1. *Ceremonial of Bishops* no. 74, footnote 67, referencing *Cæremoniale Episcoporum*, ed. 1886, I, XI, 8.

Aspersory [also called Aspersorium or Holy Water Bucket]

The Aspersory, or holy water bucket, is carried in the right hand with the left hand over your heart. Be careful not to spill the holy water. Present the Aspergill to the Priest with your left hand. Do not to let the bucket hang carelessly.

Communion Paten

The purpose of the communion paten (sometimes called "communion-plate") is to catch any crumbs that might fall, or even a dropped host. "The communion-plate for the Communion of the Faithful should be retained, so as to avoid the danger of the sacred host or some fragment of it falling."[1]

Stand to the outside of the Priest, Deacon, or Extraordinary Minister of Holy Communion and hold the plate directly under the chins of those receiving Communion on the tongue, and directly under the hands of those receiving in the hand[2].

When carrying a communion paten, always be mindful of keeping it right-side up and perfectly level. Always treat it as if it had the Body of Christ sitting on it.

When you walk with it, put your hand along the edge to shield any crumbs from falling.

When you return a communion paten to the altar or credence table after Communion, do not stack it on top of anything and do not stack anything on top of it.

THE GOSPEL PROCESSION

Even as an apprentice server, you may be called upon to participate in the Gospel Procession. There are several different forms, depending upon the solemnity of the day and the number of altar servers available. It is worthwhile for even apprentice servers to become familiar with the various forms. See page 45.

---

1. *Redemptionis Sacramentum*, no. 93.
2. Fortescue, p. 102; Elliot, *Ceremonies of the Modern Roman Rite* no. 114; *cf. Roman Missal* nos. 118 and 287, *Ceremonial of Bishops* no. 125.

HOLDING AND CARRYING THE MISSAL AND OTHER BOOKS

The Book Bearer brings the *Missal* to the M.C. (or Server 1) whenever the Priest says "Let us pray". You will learn to anticipate this, so as to arrive before the Priest as he speaks. Always carry the *Missal* with two hands.

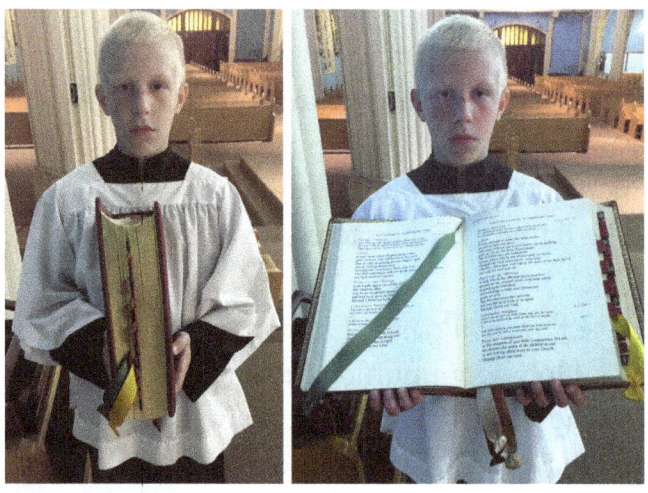

Carrying the Missal: Closed and Open

Stand in front of the Priest and hold the *Missal* high enough so that it is held at the chest level of the Priest, directly in front of him. This may require you to rest the upper edge of the *Missal* upon your forehead if the Priest is significantly taller than you!

When you carry the *Missal* stand to the altar, be careful to carry it resting against your breast with both hands supporting the underside.

Carrying a Book in Procession

On occasion, you may be asked to carry a book in procession. There are several acceptable ways of doing this, depending on the weight and thickness of the book. You cannot go wrong by carrying any book with both hands securely underneath it.

Carrying a Ritual Book in Procession

ADVANCED CEREMONIAL ACTIONS

The gestures and bodily posture of both the Priest, the Deacon, and the ministers, and also of the people, must be conducive to making the entire celebration resplendent with beauty and noble simplicity… Attention must therefore be paid to what is determined by this General Instruction and by the traditional practice of the Roman Rite and to what serves the common spiritual good of the People of God, rather than private inclination or arbitrary choice.

(General Instruction of the Roman Missal no. 42)

THERE IS MUCH TO LEARN IN serving at the altar of the Lord. Once you have mastered the basics, you should want to begin learning more. The following actions are typically performed by older and more advanced servers.

RINGING THE BELLS

Important actions in the Mass are signaled by the ringing of the altar bell or sanctus bell. The bell is rung with the right hand as follows: firmly grasp the handle of the bell, then twist it once.

Here are some rules to remember:

1. When you ring the bell, your ring should be firm and clear and not choppy.
2. Don't pick up the bell before it is time to ring it, otherwise, it will give off a tinkling sound.
3. Don't smother the bell by placing it down too quickly. Let the bell tone fade off before replacing the bell.

The bell should be rung at the specific times during the Mass[1] and other liturgies:
- During the *Sanctus*[2], each time you hear the "t" in the word "sanctus" or the "y" in the word "holy".
- At the *epiclesis*[3] (when the Priest extends both hands over the gifts at the altar): a single short, simple ring.
- At the elevations of the Consecrated Host and the Chalice[4] (depending on the custom of the parish, this can be either three long rings or three triple-rings each).
- When the Priest takes Communion from the chalice[5] (a single short, simple ring).

---

1. *General Instruction*, no. 150. See also below.
2. Fortescue, p. 101.
3. Elliott, *Ceremonies of the Modern Roman Rite*, nos. 295, 535.
4. Elliott, *Ceremonies of the Modern Roman Rite*, nos. 113, 305, 535.
5. Fortescue, pp. 83, 101–102, 118

- During Benediction, as the Priest blesses the people with the Eucharist in the monstrance[1] (three long rings or three triple-rings).
- During the *Gloria in excelsis Deo*, both on Holy Thursday[2] and the Easter Vigil[3] (continuously).

After the *Gloria* on Holy Thursday until the *Gloria* at the Easter Vigil, the altar bell is not used. Instead, the altar server uses a wooden *crotalus*. In some parishes, it is the custom to begin doing this starting the Fifth Sunday in Lent, when the statues and Crosses are veiled, with the exception of the *Gloria* on Holy Thursday, when the bell is always used.

ARRANGING THE ALTAR

Following the conclusion of the prayers of the faithful, Server 1, Server 2, and the Book Bearer walk to a position just behind the main altar in triangle formation. They bow to the altar together, the Book Bearer places the missal stand, returns to his spot behind the other servers, and then they all bow to the altar again. They continue to the credence table.

Server 1 and Server 2 bring the veiled chalice assembly to the altar. They hand the vessels to the one arranging the altar–this will be the Deacon or M.C.

If no one is arranging the altar, they place the items reverently on the altar in their proper place as follows:

Server 1 begins by placing the veiled chalice assembly on the altar to the right of the center. Server 1 removes the burse and hands it to Server 2. Server 2 opens the burse for Server 1. Server 1 removes the corporal and unfolds it, centering it on the Altar. **Do not flip the corporal over.** It is left with the creases down.

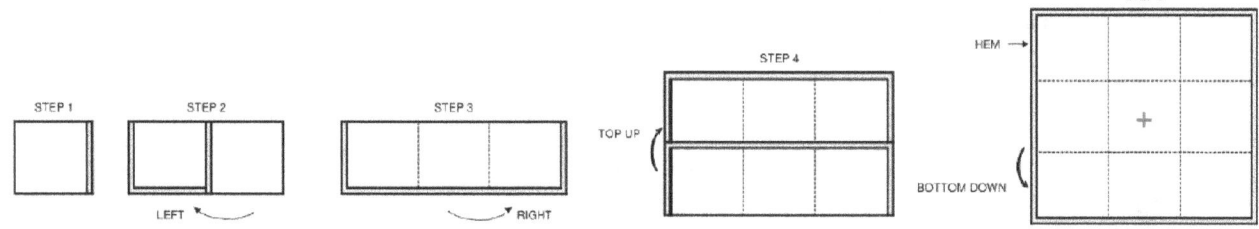

Server 1 moves the remaining chalice assembly to the top center square of the corporal. He removes the chalice veil[4] and hands it to Server 2, who folds it in thirds and places it on top of the burse.

Server 1 then places the corporal, chalice, purificator, and paten as shown on the next page.

---

1. Elliott, *Ceremonies of the Modern Roman Rite*, no. 688.
2. *Roman Missal*, page 299 no. 7.
3. *Roman Missal*, page 368 no. 31.
4. "It is a praiseworthy practice to cover the chalice with a veil, which may be either the color of the day or white" (*General Instruction,* no. 118). Its use seems to be mandatory in Pontifical Masses (*Ceremonial of Bishops,* no. 125).

Server 1 and Server 2 return to the credence table, Server 2 taking the burse and folded chalice veil with him. They then take to the Altar any other chalices and relevant vessels. If there are additional patens, chalices, and/or purificators, should be placed at the right side of the Altar on a secondary corporal as shown.

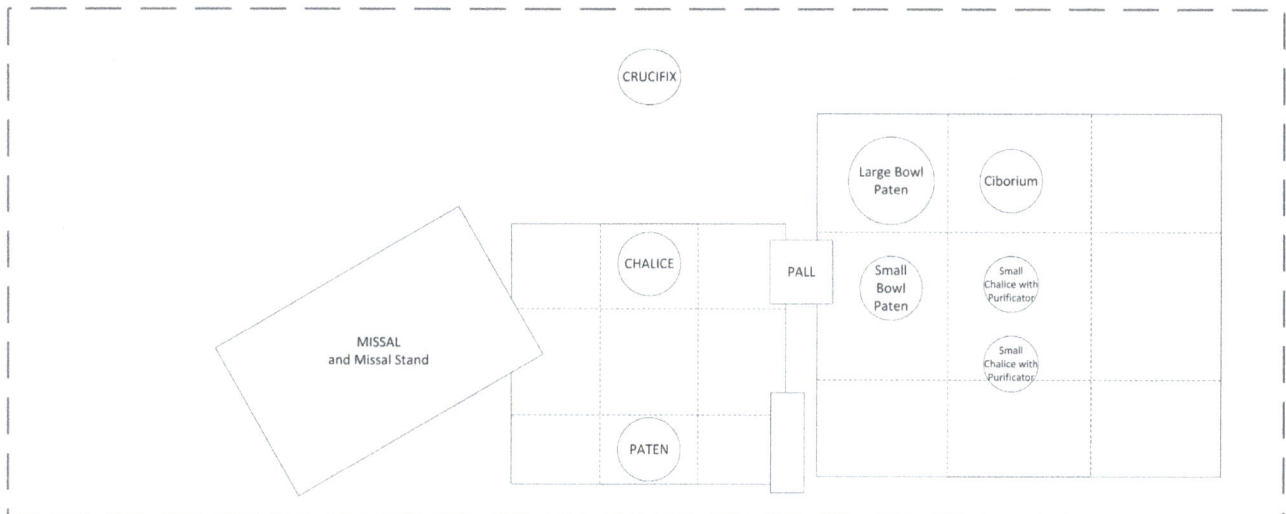

INCENSING

The thurible (or censer) is used to incense at Mass "on Sundays and festive days"[1], and in solemn ceremonies, some blessings, funerals, and at Benediction of the Blessed Sacrament. The Thurifer carries the thurible and incense boat, unless there is a dedicated Boat Bearer. The Thurifer leads most processions, since immediately behind the thurifer is the Crucifix. During Eucharistic processions, however, the Thurifer goes in front of the monstrance with the Eucharist, which is the True Presence of Christ.

Carry the thurible with your right hand with your thumb in the ring at the top and your middle finger holding the chain, so the cover is slightly raised, letting the thurible swing freely backwards and forwards. If there is no Boat Bearer, carry the incense boat in your left hand in front of you at elbow level[2].

1.   *General Instruction*, no. 119.
2.   *Ceremonial of Bishops*, no. 74, footnote 66, referencing *Cæremoniale Episcoporum*, ed. 1886, I, XI, 7.

Read over these rules and keep them in mind.

1. When genuflecting, be careful to lift the thurible so you don't bang it on the floor.

2. When walking, let the thurible swing freely. If you are not carrying the incense boat, place your unoccupied hand over your heart.

3. When presenting the open thurible for incense, be certain to hold it high enough and close enough for the Priest to reach it. The incense boat should be held right next to the open thurible.

4. When incensing someone, make a profound bow before and after you incense.

5. To incense anyone or anything: after you bow, take the chains beneath the disk with your left hand against your breast. Grasp the chains near the cover between the index finger and middle finger of your right hand. Now lift the thurible to a height just below your eyes, then swing it toward the object or person in a double or single swing. Remember to lower the thurible after each double or single swing. Be careful of the chains or you may get them tangled.

6. Take care to incense "with a grave and graceful"[1] demeanor. Keep your head and body still and don't bobble around. Keep a measured beat.

7. In incensing, there are two kinds of swings—the double swing (or *ductus*) and the single swing (or *ictus*). The outward movement is called the "throw". For a "double swing", there are two "throws", or two outward motions. For a "single swing", there is one "throw", or one outward motion[2]. The single and double swings may be given in sets of one, two, or three.

1. *Ceremonial of Bishops*, no. 91, footnote 75, referencing *Cæremoniale Episcoporum*, ed. 1886, I, XXIII, 8.
2. Elliott, *Ceremonies of the Modern Roman Rite*, no. 217.

How Many Swings Should Be Used[1]

How Many Swings?	What are you incensing?
Three Double Swings[1]	The Blessed Sacrament.
	Relic of the True Cross.
	An image of the Lord, solemnly exposed.
	The Celebrant.
	A Concelebrant or group of Concelebrants.
	The Cross.
Two Double Swings	Relics and images of the saints, solemnly exposed.
	The Deacon.
Three Single Swings	The Choir (when together).
	The Altar Servers or Torchbearers (if there are three or more in a group).
	The Congregation.
One Single Swing	M.C.
	Any other individual.

Incense is used during the entrance procession, the Gospel, the preparation of the gifts, and during the Eucharistic prayer[2]. The Thurifer should make sure that the charcoals are still lit during the Responsorial Psalm, and during the start of the homily.

---

1. *Ceremonial of Bishops*, no. 92; Elliott, *Ceremonies of the Modern Roman Rite*, nos. 218, 397, 403.
1. Despite the custom, prevalent in some places, of swinging the thurible in different directions for each of the three swings, this is not envisioned in either the rubrics or in the Tradition. See "The Correct Use of Incense at Holy Mass and other Liturgies" *Archdiocese of Portland in Oregon Divine Worship Newsletter*, April 2019.
2. *General Instruction*, nos. 49, 75, 119, 120a, 123, 132–135, 144, 150, 173–175, 178, 179, 190, 211, 212; summarized in 276–277.

SERVER MOVEMENT DIAGRAMS

There should be harmony and diligence among all those involved in the effective preparation of each liturgical celebration in accordance with the Missal and other liturgical books, both as regards the rites and as regards the pastoral and musical aspects.

(General Instruction of the Roman Missal, no. 111)

DIAGRAMS FOR THE VARIOUS PARTS OF the Mass are found here. In some cases, there are several different ways for things to be done, and in your parish you may have made changes based on the specific layout of your church and sanctuary. In addition, various diagrams for different options for the Entrance Procession and Gospel Procession are given. If you are a new server, or if you are serving in an unfamiliar church, you should always ask the M.C., Priest, or a responsible server to explain the customs of the place you are serving.

See also: "Appendix 2: Serving Ad Orientem" on page 114 and "Appendix 3: Vespers" on page 121.

KEY TO SYMBOLS IN THE DIAGRAMS

	Thurifer		C	Celebrant
	Boat Bearer		Cc	Concelebrant
	Cross Bearer		D	Deacon
S₁ S₂	Server 1, Server 2		D₁ D₂	Deacon 1, Deacon 2 (when more than one)
	Book Bearer		B	Bishop
or Cₙ	Candle Bearer		Mb Cb	Miter Bearer / Crozier Bearer
	Torchbearer		E	Extraordinary Minister of Holy Communion (EMHC)
MC	Master of Ceremonies		L	Lector

DIRECTIONS IN THE SANCTUARY

It is the duty of every altar server to become familiar with the sanctuary of their parish church. Each one is different: the sanctuary in the diagrams may not match yours!

Since directions like "left" or "right" depend on which way you are facing, we are using standard liturgical directions in our instructions, as indicated in the diagram below. Liturgical East is always towards where the high altar and tabernacle are traditionally located, even if that direction is not really east according to a compass.

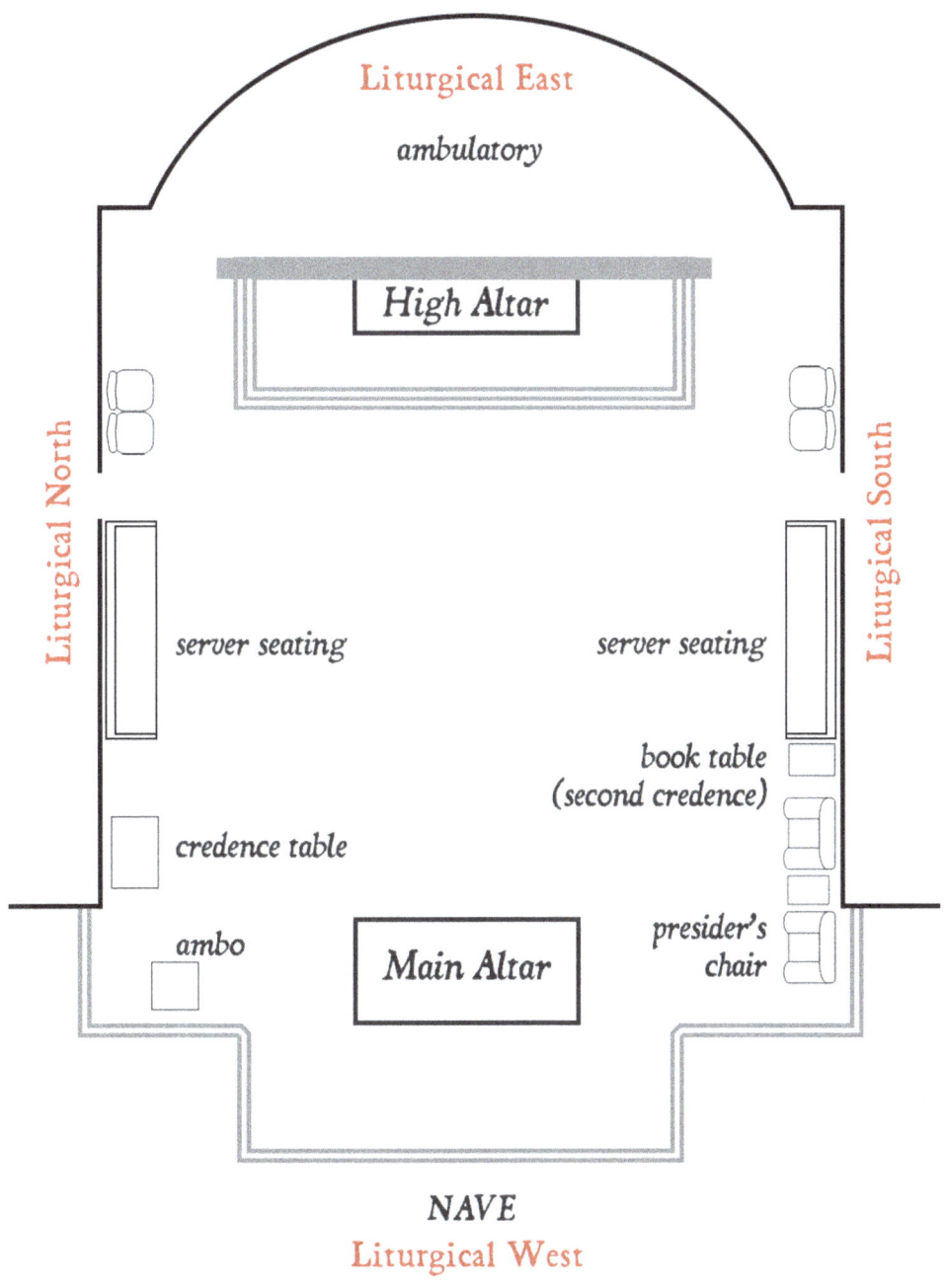

1: Various Forms of Entrance Procession

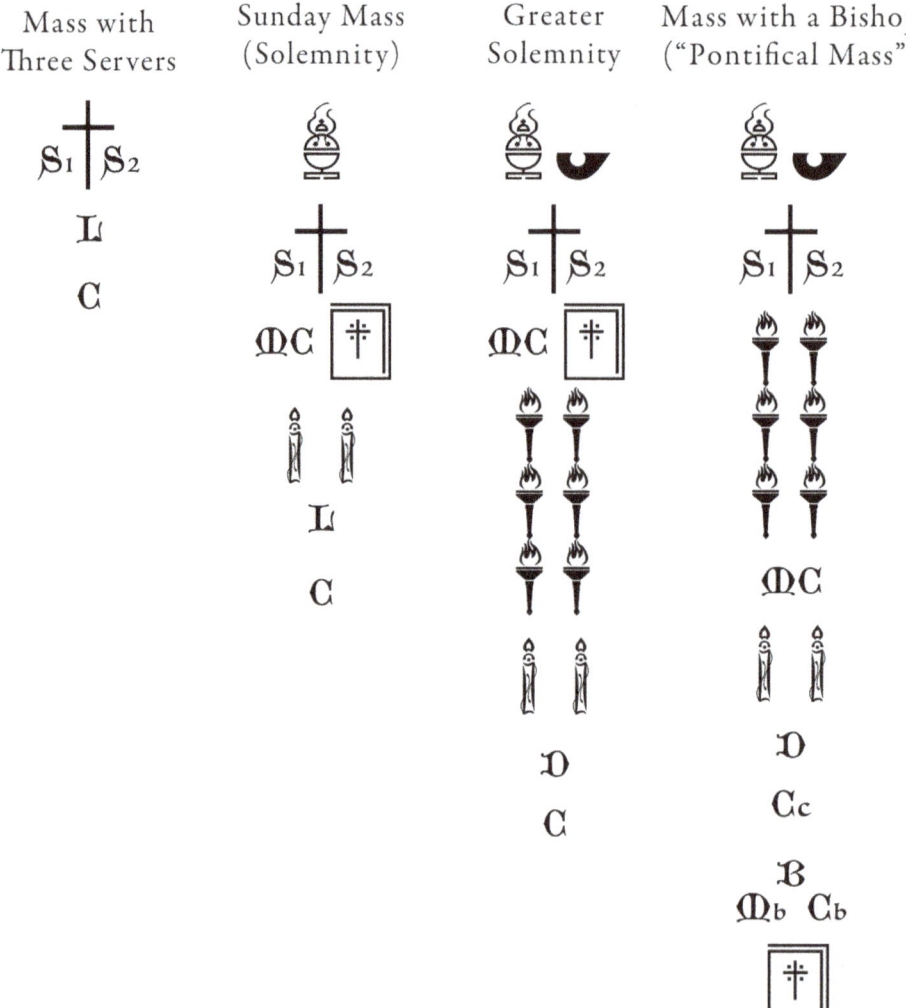

Mass with Three Servers | Sunday Mass (Solemnity) | Greater Solemnity | Mass with a Bishop ("Pontifical Mass")

2: ARRIVAL AT THE FOOT OF THE ALTAR

Option A: Entering Immediately

As each group or pair of servers arrive at the entrance to the sanctuary, they genuflect or bow as appropriate and then enter the sanctuary to repose their items and go to their seats. The Thurifer, Boat Bearer, and M.C. take up their positions as shown in "3: Preparing for the Introductory Rites".

Option B: Lining Up at the Foot

As each group or pair of servers arrive at the entrance to the sanctuary, they sweep to take up their position as indicated in the diagram and face the sanctuary. Once the Celebrant arrives, all together genuflect or bow as appropriate. They continue as shown in "3: Preparing for the Introductory Rites".

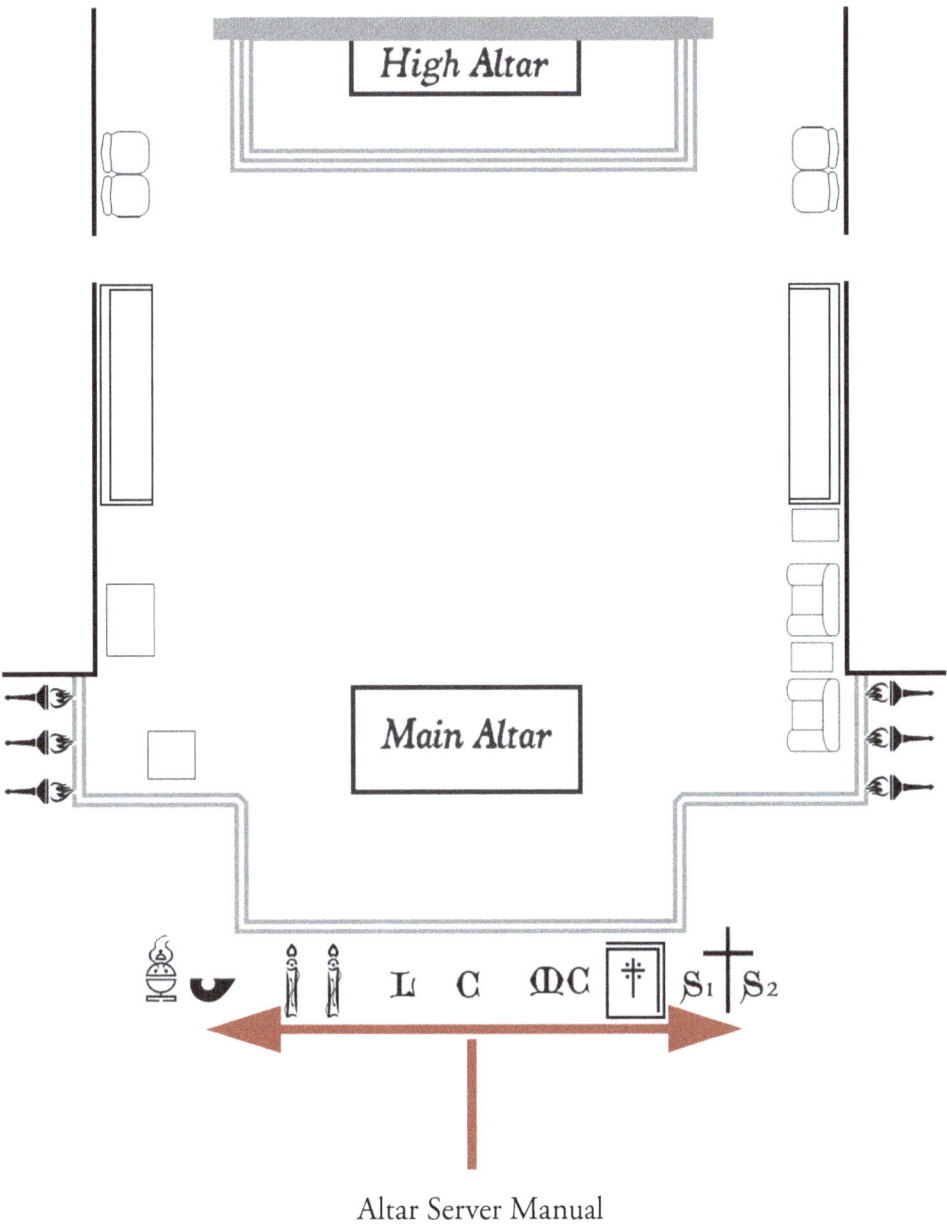

3: Preparing for the Introductory Rites

How to Enter the Sanctuary from the Foot

If Option 2B on the previous page is taken, after bowing or genuflecting, the servers continue as indicated in the diagram.

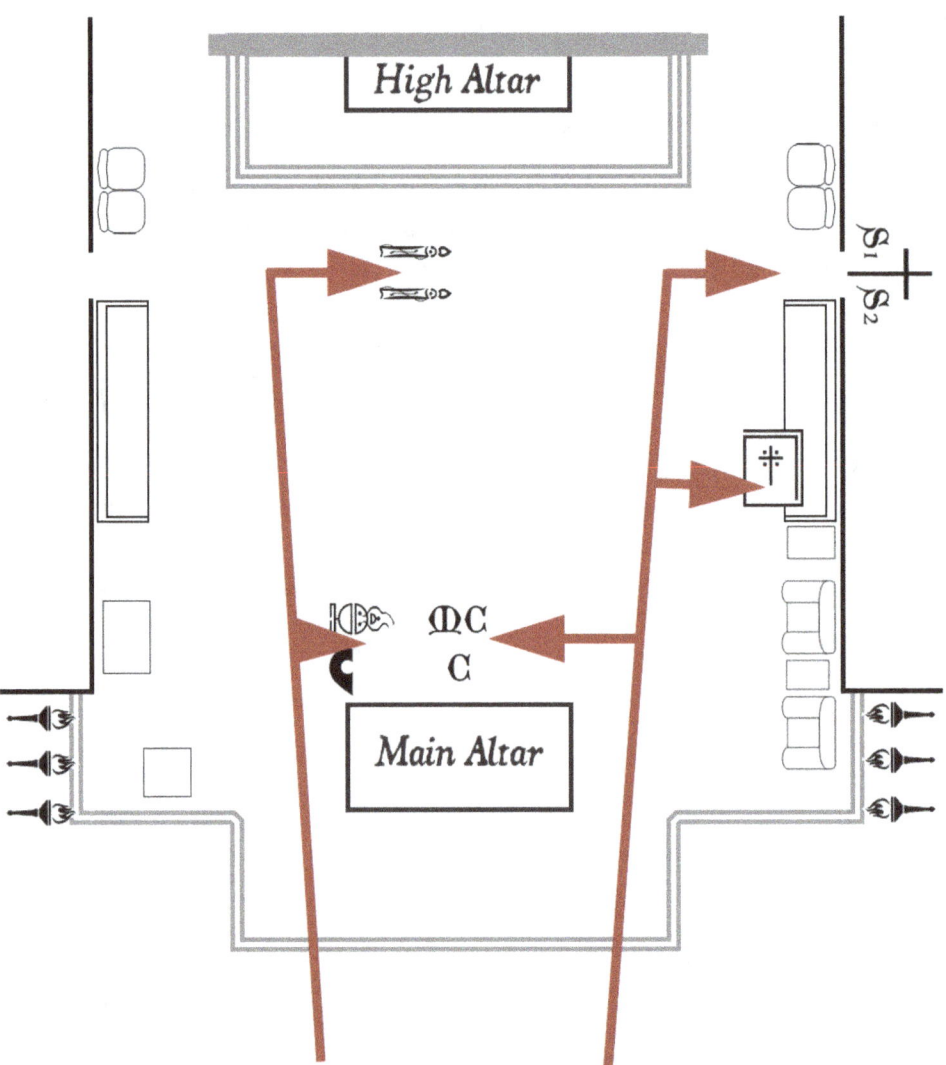

1. All take one step back to allow Thurifer / Boat Bearer to go first.
2. Once Thurifer approaches the altar, the Cross and candles formation goes next.
3. Outside groups go next (M.C. / Book Bearer and Candle Bearer pair).
4. Progressively inward groups follow, pair by pair.
5. Torchbearers go last, in two single file columns (see illustration on next page). They should not begin moving into the sanctuary until the Candlebearers have begun their transit of the high altar.

Preparing for Introductory Rites / Torchbearers

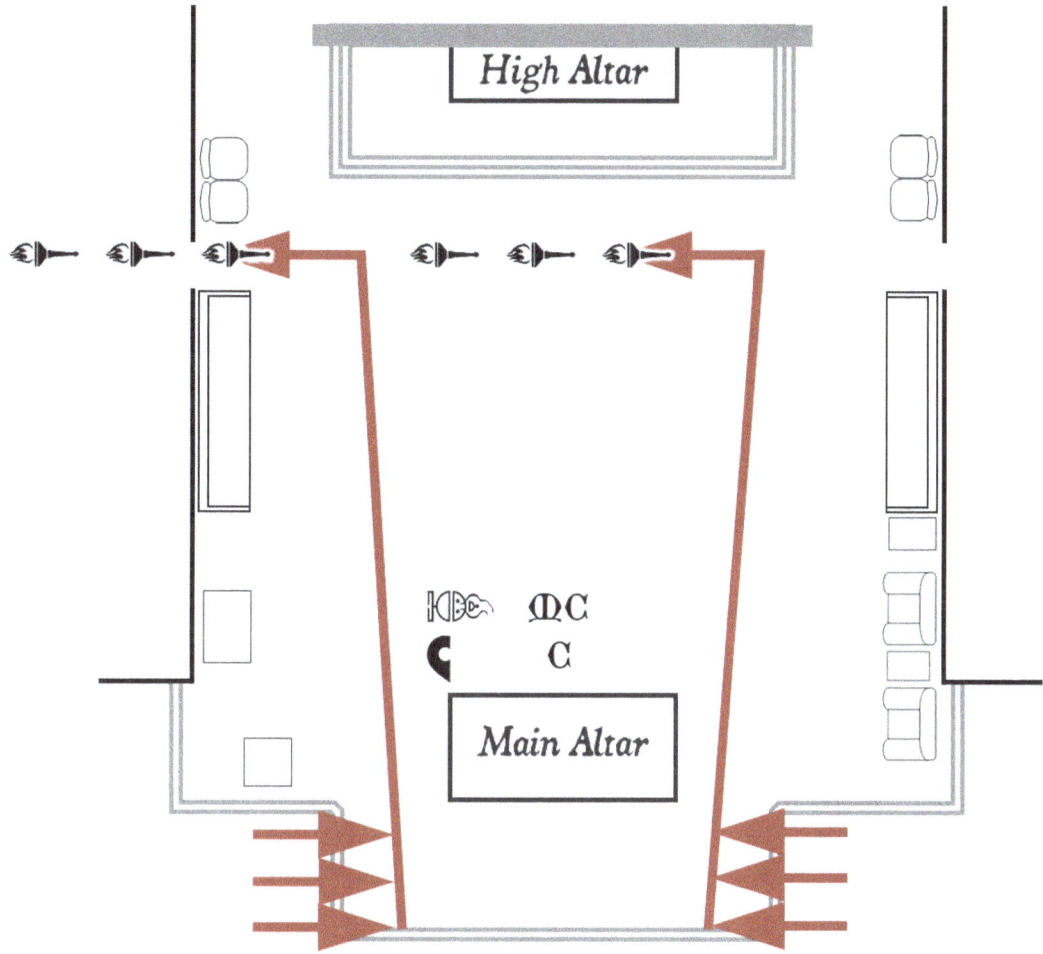

NOTE: If it is at all possible for the Candles and South Torches to enter the sacristies through the ambulatory, they should do so to avoid crossing in front of the tabernacle.

If the Candle Bearers do cross in front of the tabernacle (as pictured in diagram 3), they must remember to sweep to face the tabernacle, bow, and then sweep back and continue to the sacristy. Torchbearers, since they are moving in single file, will not need to sweep, but they must still stop, turn, bow, then turn and continue.

Reposing the Cross and Candles

The place of reposing the Cross and candles varies by parish. Candlebearers will almost always repose their candles in a sacristy. For the candles carried by Servers 1 and 2, there are generally three options. Your trainer or M.C. will advise you of which option is used in your parish.

1. Candles are reposed on or near main altar, where they remain lit.
2. Candles are reposed on a credence table, where they remain lit.
3. Candles are reposed in the sacristy, where they are extinguished.

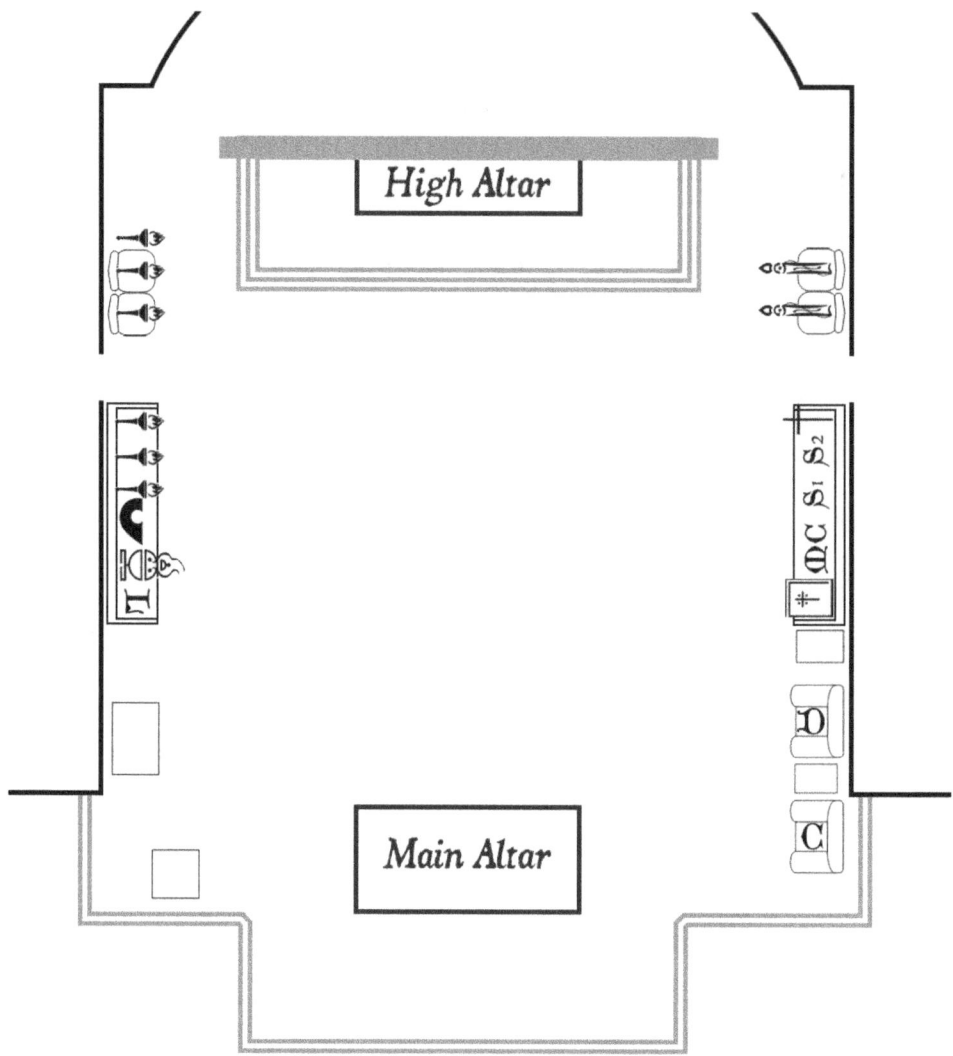

The seating plan for servers at your parish may vary, depending on the available seating in the sanctuary, whether or not the Lector(s) sit in the sanctuary, if there are concelebrating Priests or additional Deacons, etc. Even on this diagram, you can see we'll need to pull out an additional chair or we'll have a standing Torchbearer throughout Mass!

The M.C. should have a clear line of sight, if possible, to all those ministering in the Mass. The M.C. will supervise the Altar Servers on the south side of the sanctuary and help the Priest or Deacon if necessary. The Thurifer will perform the same functions for the north side of the sanctuary.

It's often helpful to have a credence table on both sides of the sanctuary. The one on the south side will hold the *Missal* and its stand, as well as the server candles if your parish chooses this option. The one on the north side will contain the chalice assembly, lavabo dish, purificators, and communion patens.

5: Various Forms of the Gospel Procession

There are several different forms of Gospel Procession, depending upon the solemnity of the day and the number of altar servers available. We will begin with the most solemn (and complicated) and work our way down to daily Mass with a single altar server.

Depending on the layout of your sanctuary, your M.C. or Trainer may have a slightly different procedure for the start of these processions.

In all cases the signal for the altar server or servers to begin the procession is the beginning of the *Alleluia* or *verse before the Gospel.*

5a: The Four-Candle Procession (with Thurifer)

In the four-candle procession, Server 1, Server 2, the Candle Bearers, the Thurifer, and (if present) the Boat Bearer and M.C. stand together at the beginning of the third antiphon of the Responsorial Psalm, usually at a signal from the M.C., and proceed to the sacristy to light their candles and obtain the thurible and boat.

NOTE: If there are lit candles at the Credence table, Server 1 and Server 2 will take them in hand and wait for the start of the procession, where they will follow the Thurifer as he passes them. The Candle Bearers will fall in behind them. Although it sounds complicated, with a little practice this will become a smooth procedure.

The order of the procession is: Thurifer (with Boat Bearer), followed by Servers 1 and 2 with lit candles, followed by the Candle Bearers with lit candles, followed by M.C. (if any),

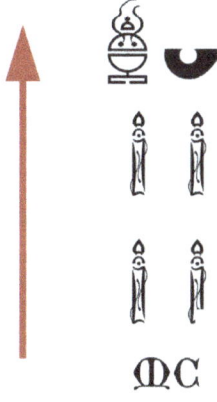

Order of the Gospel Procession

Processing from the South to the Presider's Chair

The preferred start of the procession is from the south. Proceed directly to the Presider's Chair, with the Thurifer (and Boat Bearer) in front of the Priest (and Deacon if any), while the rest wait a few steps back.

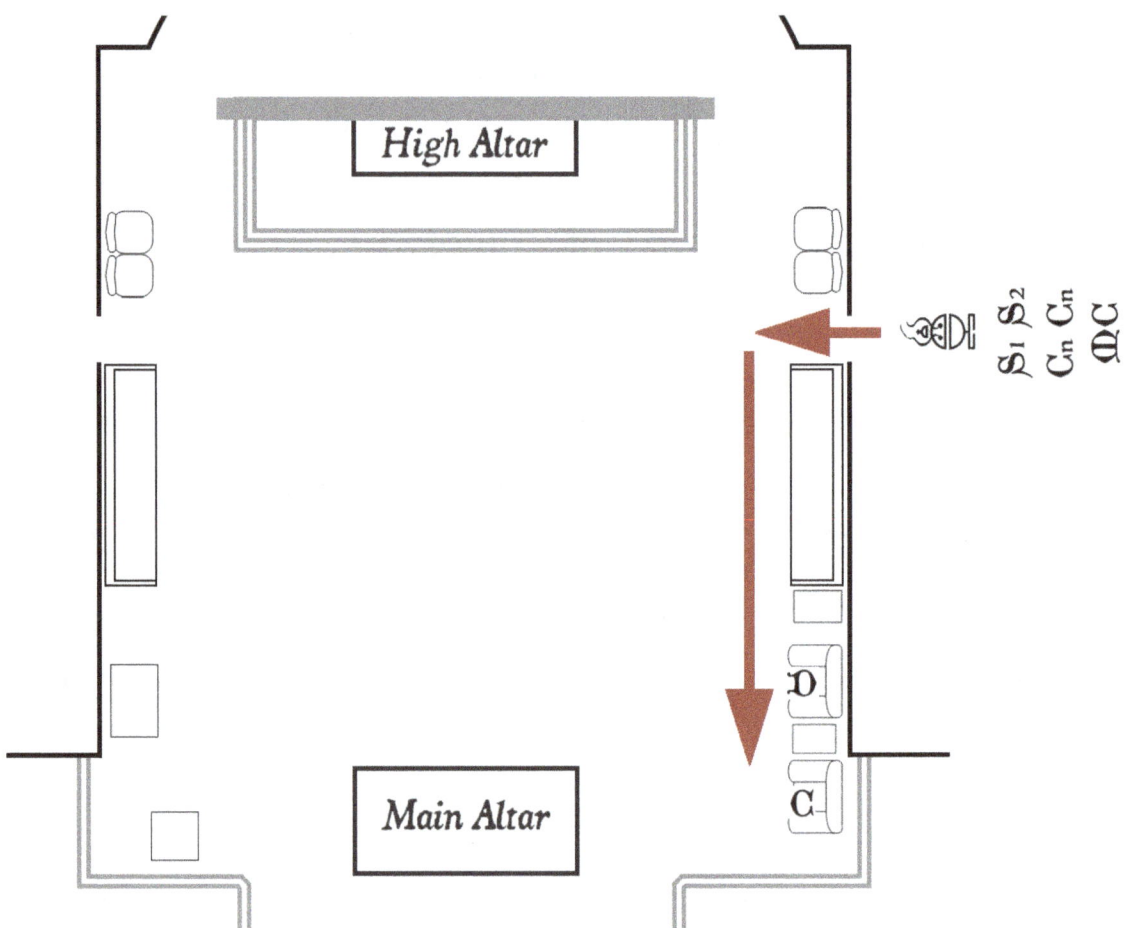

Preferred Option: from the South

Processing from the North to the Presider's Chair

If the layout of your church requires it, you may process from the north instead. Proceed through the ambulatory to the Presider's Chair, with the Thurifer (and Boat Bearer) in front of the Priest (and Deacon if any), while the rest wait a few steps back.

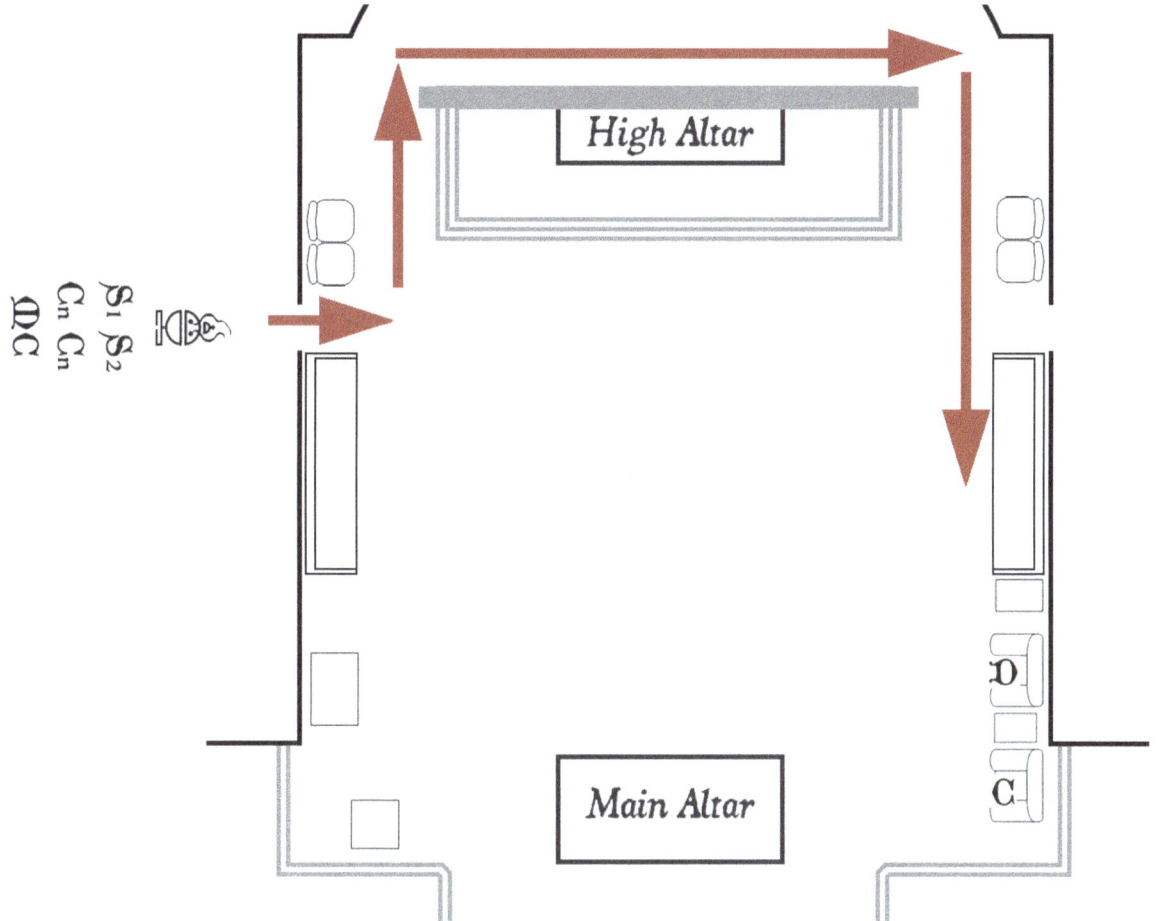

Alternate Option: from the North

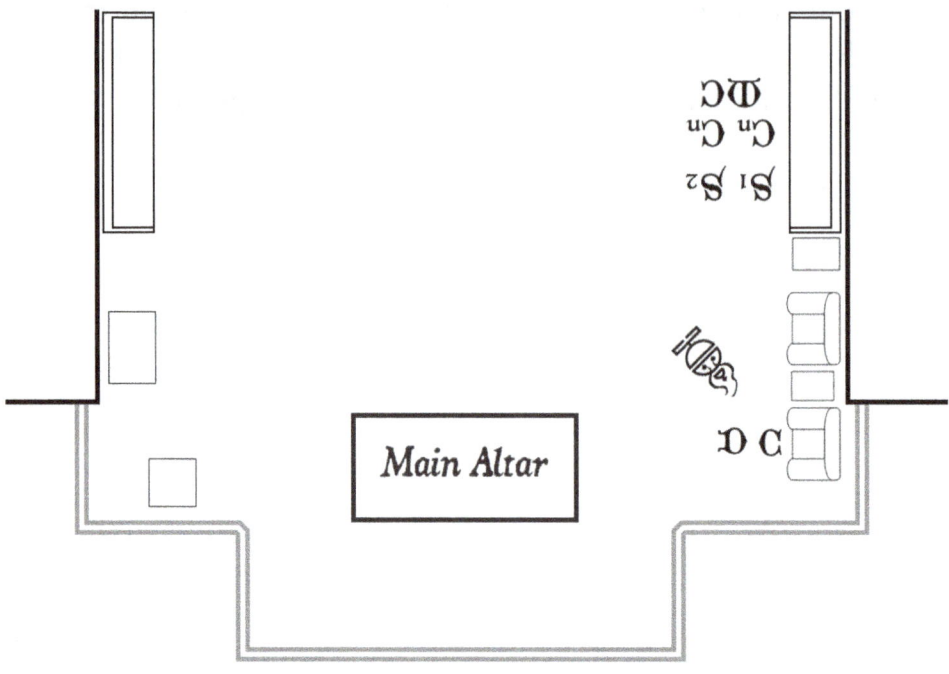

The Priest Imposes Incense

Once incense has been imposed, proceed to the altar. The Candle Bearers must remember to make room for the Priest (or Deacon) in front of them!

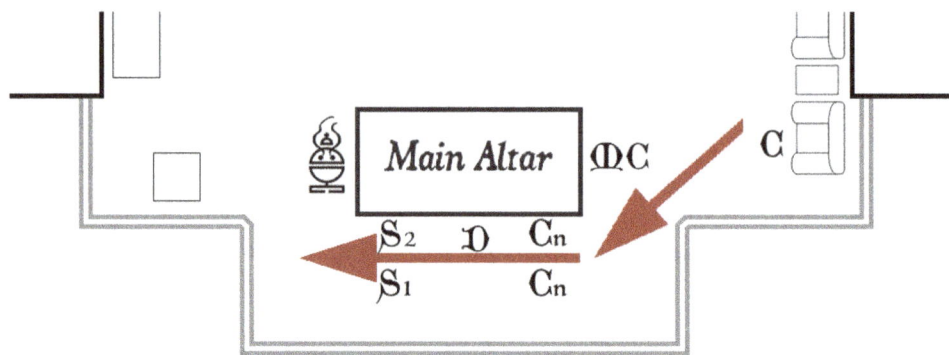

The Gospel Procession from the Presider's Chair to the Main Altar

Note that when the altar servers turn to face the altar, they do *not* turn in a sweep as normal, but pivot in place.

Four-Candle Gospel Procession and the Proclamation of the Gospel

From the Altar to the Ambo

When the Priest or Deacon, having held up the *Book of the Gospels*, turns toward the ambo, all likewise turn to face the ambo, and all proceed to the ambo.

Candle Bearers and Server 1 / Server 2 take up their positions on either side of the Ambo, sweeping as necessary. Thurifer, Boat Bearer, and M.C. take up their position several steps behind the Priest or Deacon.

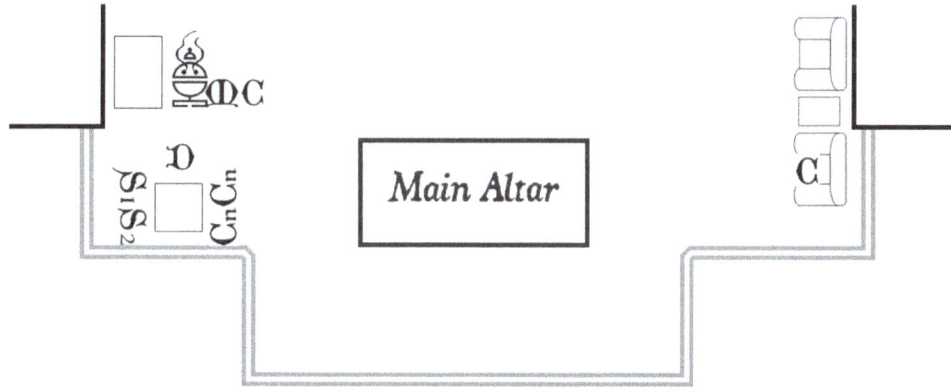

The Proclamation of the Gospel (Four Candles)

After the Gospel

At the words "the Gospel of the Lord", respond "Praise to you, Lord Jesus Christ." Then, turn towards the sacristy, and return there by the shortest route.

5b: The Two-Candle Procession (with or without Thurifer)

The two-candle procession is similar to the four-candle procession, but with a little twist.

Following the imposition of incense (if there is a Thurifer), the pair of altar servers walks past the Priest (and Deacon) to the center of the main altar. There, they bow, then they separate and take up their positions at the corners of the altar.

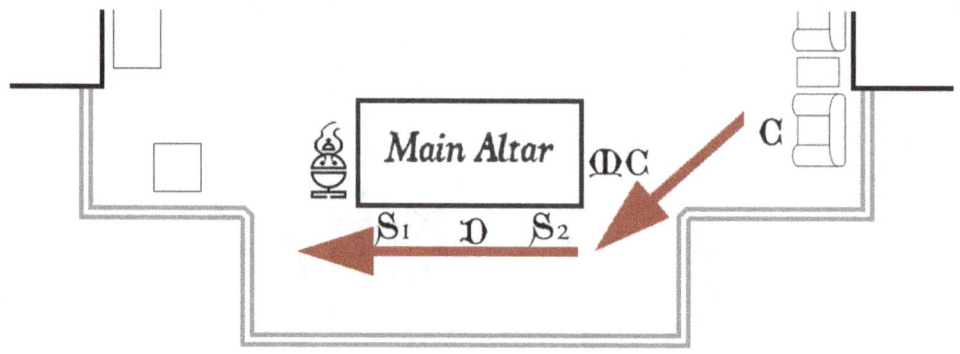

Two-Candle Gospel Procession

All proceeds as with the four-candle procession, with both altar servers *in front of and leading* the Priest or Deacon as they walk to the ambo. At the ambo, each altar server takes their position on either side of the ambo.

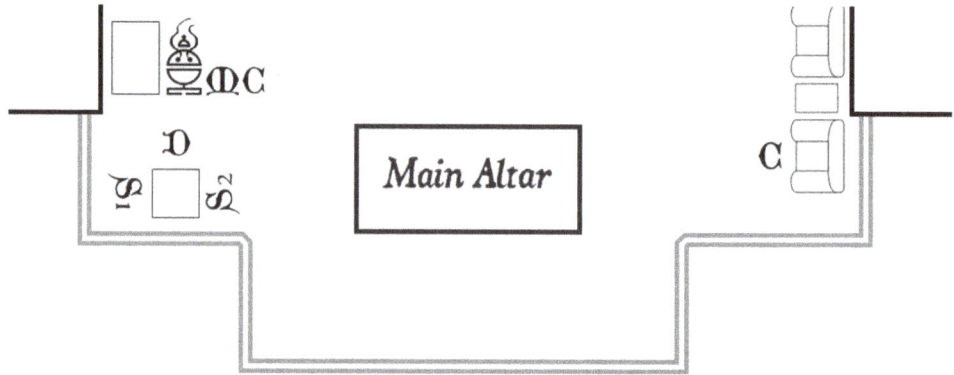

The Proclamation of the Gospel (Two Candles)

5c: One or Two Candles at Daily Mass

Daily Mass is normally celebrated with a single server (or at most two servers). If there are two servers, the preferred option is to use the two-candle procession as above. If there is only one server, the Gospel procession is greatly simplified.

Lit candle in hand, enter the sanctuary and stop. Wait a moment for the lector to leave the ambo, at which point, go to the north side of the ambo and await the Priest or Deacon.

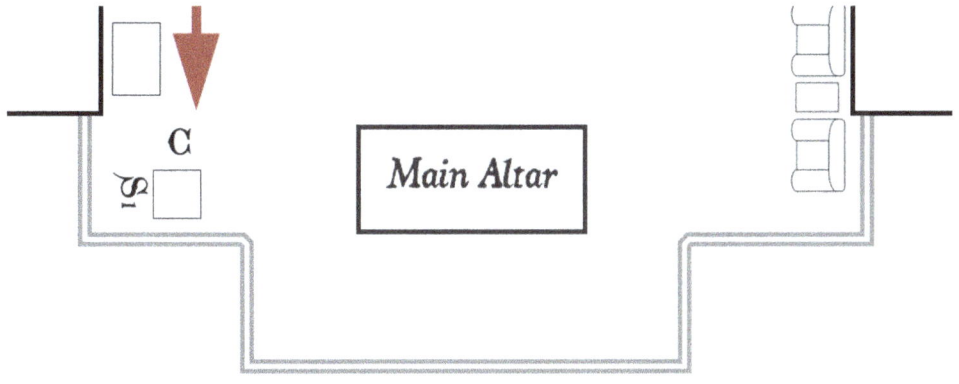

Gospel Ambo Position for Daily Mass

6: READY POSITION

When assisting during the different stages of the offertory, Servers 1 and 2 will often need to wait or pause while the Priest is praying. They remain in the "ready position" near to the credence table and behind the ambo until required.

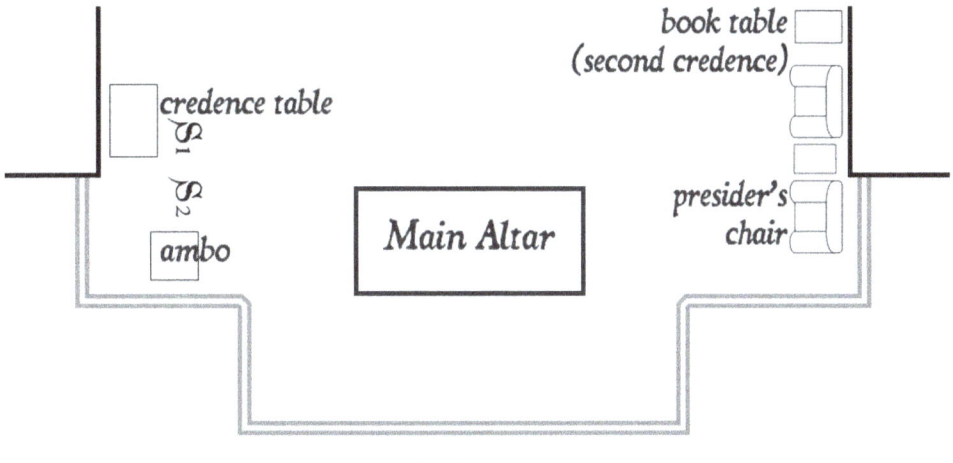

Ready Position

7: Eucharistic Prayer (After *Sanctus*)

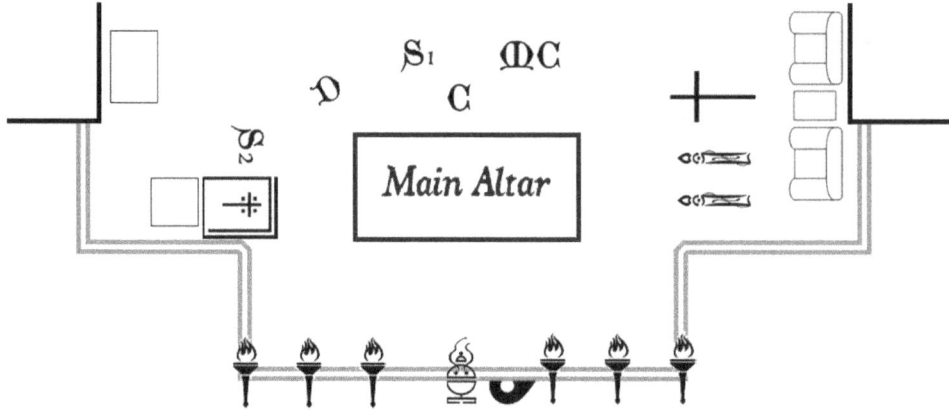

8: Initial Server Communion Position

Servers 1 and 2 fetch the communion patens and stand at the ready, one with the Extraordinary Ministers of Holy Communion, and one with the servers. Torchbearers flank the sanctuary at the steps. The remaining servers and M.C. line up behind the altar.

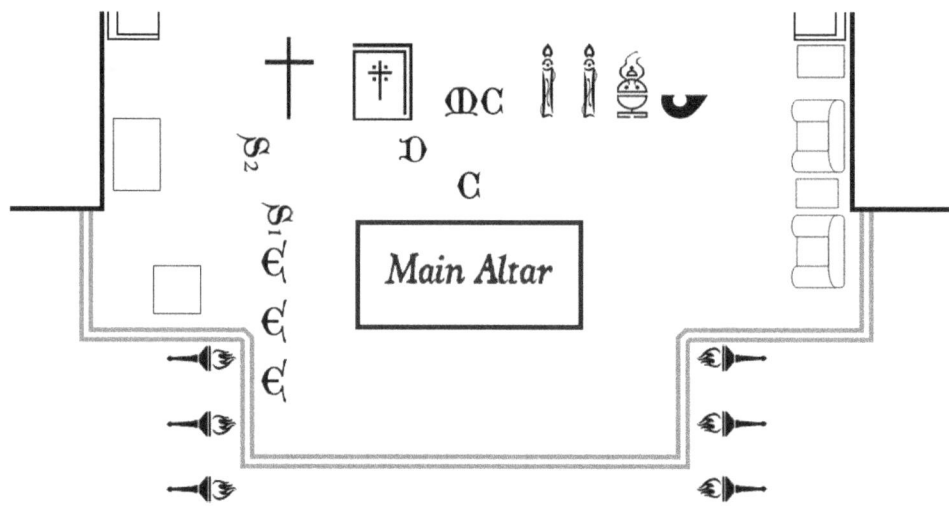

Once the servers, M.C., and EMHCs have received Communion, S1 attends the Priest and S2 the EMHC. The M.C. gives the Cross Bearer and Thurifer purificators so that they may stand watch. The Book Bearer reposes the missal stand.

Torchbearers maintain their position throughout the entirety of the Communion Rite and only retire when the Eucharist is reposed. They walk in and out in single file, using the same route as found on page 43 to return to the sacristy.

Remaining servers return to their seats and stand for the duration of Communion.

9: Leaving the Sanctuary: the Recessional

Preparation
1. Cross Bearer, Server 1, and Server 2 fetch Cross and candles after final blessing.
2. If it is the custom at your parish, all kneel during Saint Michael Prayer.
3. Cross Bearer, Server 1, and Server 2 come down when music begins and take their position in the center aisle at the third pew.
4. Others begin moving only when the Priest Celebrant does.
5. Line up at foot of altar on the same side your seat was.
6. If applicable, M.C. fetches biretta and takes their place next to Celebrant at the step.
7. At signal from M.C. or Celebrant, all genuflect. (Cross and Candles head bow.)
8. M.C. hands Celebrant his biretta and all turn around.

Leaving the Step of the Altar
1. South side outside pair first.
2. Then north side outside pair.
3. Alternate pairs, side to side, until done.
4. Clergy go last.

Religious Sisters

Sodalities, Associations, etc.
(with banners)

Clergy

Knights of Columbus

CHOIR

People

If there are additional servers (to swap out with the Torchbearers or Baldachin Bearers if they get tired, for example), they walk immediately behind the baldachin (canopy).

Altar Server Duties

"The liturgy is the celebration of the mystery of Christ, given to the Church, in which we are called to enter with always greater intensity, also in virtue of the ever-new and providential repetitiousness of the rite."

— Bishop Guido Marini,
Master of Pontifical Liturgical Celebrations (2007–2021)

DURING THE MASS, EACH PERSON in the sanctuary has a specific job to do. Altar servers are no different. In a basic team of four altar servers, there will be a Cross Bearer, a Book Bearer, and two altar servers called Server 1 and Server 2. Each of them has a different set of duties during the Mass. In a team of three, the Cross Bearer will also take the Book Bearer's responsibilities.

For some Masses, additional altar servers will be assigned. For Sundays and Solemnities, there will also be a Thurifer and two Candle Bearers (who may also serve as Torchbearers) and perhaps additional Torchbearers. For Masses with a Bishop, which are called "Pontifical Masses", there will also be a Miter Bearer and a Crozier Bearer.

Duties of All Altar Servers Before Mass

The following duties apply to all altar servers:
- At home, dress in the proper clothes and footwear for Mass as described in "Appropriate Dress" on page 15. If not properly dressed, the altar server may not be allowed to serve at that Mass.
- Arrive in the sacristy **30 minutes before Mass** is scheduled to begin.
- Upon arrival for Mass or other liturgies, sign in and check off your name on the schedule in the sacristy so that the M.C. and the Celebrant knows you have arrived. (If you are not scheduled to serve, check with the M.C. or the Celebrant to see if altar servers are needed.)
- Vest in the alb and cincture *or* cassock and surplice as instructed, praying the appropriate vesting prayers.

Duties of All Altar Servers During Mass

The duties of all Servers during and after Mass may be found in "Introduction to Mass Duty Sheets" on page 56. Each job has its own "Duty Sheet" that goes over their specific duties in detail.

Standing Watch

Two servers[1], normally the Cross Bearer and the Thurifer, will be asked to "stand watch". There are two parts to this: (1) in parishes where it is the custom, placing and removing the kneelers (prie-dieux), and (2) guarding the Eucharist from desecration.

After you receive Communion, move kneelers in the place where the Priest and other Minister will distribute Communion, so that those people who wish to receive Communion keeling may more easily do so[2].

Return to the altar so that the M.C. can give you a purificator. Your job during Communion is to watch the distribution of Communion. If the Precious Body falls to the floor, or the Precious Blood spills, you are to immediately cover the spot with your purificator, consuming the host if necessary. Then get the attention of the M.C. or Sacristan so that they can supervise the proper purification of the spot.[3]

If you ever see someone walk away with the Precious Body and not consume it, bring it to the attention of the Priest, Deacon, or M.C. immediately.

After the Communion Rite, return the kneelers to their proper positions.

DUTIES OF ALL ALTAR SERVERS AFTER MASS

Before you divest, always ask the M.C. or Priest if there is anything else you can do.

When you divest, make sure to hang your vestments properly and in the correct place. The hangers for both albs and cassocks are arranged by size so that you can more easily find the vestment you need quickly. This system only works when everybody puts their vestments away properly!

INTRODUCTION TO MASS DUTY SHEETS

The remainder of this chapter contains duty sheets for altar server positions within the Mass–Additional Servers, Altar Servers 1 and 2, Boat Bearer, Book Bearer, Candle Bearer, Cross Bearer, Thurifer, Torchbearer, Crozier and Miter Bearer—as well as one for the M.C. and one for how to serve daily Mass. Know your job!

---

1. Technically one for each Minister of Communion for the Precious Body. In Masses where there are more (or fewer) Communion stations, there will be correspondingly more or fewer watchers.
2. *Cf. General Instruction*, no. 160, referencing *Redemptionis Sacramentum*, no. 91: "The norm established for the Dioceses of the United States of America is that Holy Communion is to be received standing, unless an individual member of the faithful wishes to receive Communion while kneeling".
3. *Cf. General Instruction*, no. 280.

Before Mass

Arrive 30 minutes before Mass, and sign in and vest, saying the vesting prayers.

Entrance Procession

Processing is always done solemnly, at a moderate pace, and with a distance of three pews between each group of altar servers.

If your parish is using "Option B: Lining Up at the Foot" on page 41: when you arrive at the foot of the altar, turn towards your right or left and line up as shown in the diagram.

After you genuflect or bow, proceed up the steps.

If you have a candle, go to the sacristy as shown in "How to Enter the Sanctuary from the Foot" on page 42. Place the candles on the sacristy table and blow them out. Proceed to your seat and remain standing for the Introductory Rites.

If you do not have a candle, proceed immediately to your seat and remain standing for the Introductory Rites.

Liturgy of the Word

Listen attentively to the readings, saying the usual responses. Sing the Responsorial Psalm. Stand for the Gospel as normal. Listen attentively to the homily.

Liturgy of the Eucharist

Offertory

After being incensed by the Thurifer, turn and walk in single file to your positions as seen in "7: Eucharistic Prayer (After Sanctus)" on page 52.

Communion

After the Priest has taken his communion, all altar servers walk single file to the positions indicated in "8: Initial Server Communion Position" on page 52.

After the Priest and Server 1 and Server 2 have walked to the foot of the altar to distribute Communion to the faithful, return to stand at your seats.

Recessional

Proceed to the foot of the altar, taking the same positions you took at the start of the Mass. Turn, face the sanctuary, and wait for the Priest. Make the appropriate reverence in unison with the Priest.

Turn and walk shoulder to shoulder. See "9: Leaving the Sanctuary: the Recessional" on page 53 for more information.

ALTAR SERVER 1 AND ALTAR SERVER 2

Server 1 and Server 2 carry their processional candles during Mass for the entrance procession, the Gospel procession, and the recessional. They help receive the gifts, prepare the altar, and assist the Priest during the Liturgy of the Eucharist.

Before Mass

Arrive 30 minutes before Mass, and complete these tasks within the first fifteen minutes:
- Sign in and be vested, having said the vesting prayers.
- At fifteen minutes before the Mass is to begin, light the altar candles.

Note Be sure the correct number of altar candles are lit. For more information, see "Progressive Solemnity" on page 11.

If a seventh candle is present behind the crucifix, Server 1 lights that candle first.

Facing the tabernacle, Server 1 and Server 2 light the candles on either side, starting with the candle closest to the tabernacle. Together they proceed to the main altar and light the candles there. Candles are always lit using lucifers.

Entrance Procession

Server 1 and Server 2 process shoulder to shoulder with the Cross Bearer. Processing is always done solemnly, at a moderate pace, and with a distance of three pews between each group of altar servers.

If your parish is using "Option B: Lining Up at the Foot" on page 41: when you arrive at the foot of the altar, turn towards your right and line up as shown in "2: Arrival at the Foot of the Altar" on page 41.

After you bow, proceed up the steps with the Cross Bearer as shown in "3: Preparing for the Introductory Rites" on page 42. Place the candles in their appropriate spot.

All altar servers walk to their seats. Remain standing for the Introductory Rites.

Liturgy of the Word

Gospel Procession

At the beginning of the third antiphon of the Responsorial Psalm, the Thurifer, Boat Bearer, Server 1, Server 2, and two Candle Bearers rise from their seats and walk to the sacristy.

As the *Alleluia* or *verse before the Gospel* begins, follow the Thurifer to the Priest and wait a few steps short of the Presider's Chair. See "5a: The Four-Candle Procession (with Thurifer)" on page 45.

Once the Priest imposes the incense, proceed to the altar and take your position.

When the Priest or Deacon, having held up the *Book of the Gospels*, turns toward the Ambo, you likewise turn to face the Ambo, and all proceed as shown in "From the Altar to the Ambo" on page 49.

Server 1, Server 2, and Candle Bearers take up their positions on either side of the Ambo while the Priest or Deacon proclaims the Gospel.

At the words "the Gospel of the Lord", respond "Praise to you, Lord Jesus Christ." Then, turn towards the sacristy, and return there, shoulder to shoulder, following the Thurifer. Return your candles to their place.

Return to your seats, all sitting at the same time, and listen attentively to the remainder of the homily.

Liturgy of the Eucharist

Following the conclusion of the prayers of the faithful, Server 1 and Server 2, accompanied by the Book Bearer in triangle formation, walk to just behind the main altar. All bow to the altar. The Book Bearer places the missal stand, returns to his spot in the formation, and all bow to the altar together again.

If there is no separate Book Bearer, or if the Cross Bearer has not taken the Book Bearer's place, Server 1 places the missal stand.

They continue to the credence table.

Offertory

Server 1 and Server 2 bring to the altar the vested chalice assembly, any smaller chalices, and all other relevant vessels. Hand the vessels to the one arranging the altar. If no one is arranging the altar, place the items reverently on the altar in their proper place. In this case, Server 1 will prepare the altar and Server 2 will assist.

After the altar has been arranged, Server 1 and Server 2 stand in the ready position. When the Priest comes forward, accompany him to the foot of the altar to assist in receiving the gifts. The Priest hands Server 1 and Server 2 the bread and wine offerings.

The sacred vessel holding the unconsecrated bread is brought to the altar. After handing the bread to the one arranging the altar (or placing it on a corporal on the altar if there is no one arranging the altar), the altar servers continue together to the credence table to fetch the water cruet.

Remove the stoppers on the wine and water cruets and place the stoppers on the credence table. Server 1 holds the wine and Server 2 holds the water cruet. Hold the cruet at the base in your right hand, at heart level, with the handle facing away from you. Turn around and proceed to the side of the altar.

When the Priest faces you, together make a simple bow. Server 1 presents the wine first. Server 1 receives the cruet back. Server 2 then presents the water cruet and receives it back. Server 1 and Server 2 make a simple bow, turn around, and return to the credence table.

Prepare the lavabo items as soon as you return to the credence table.

Lavabo

Facing the credence table, Server 1 picks up the lavabo bowl and the water cruet. Server 2 unfolds the towel and carries it between his fingers. Server 1 and Server 2 turn around and approach the side of the altar. If the altar is being incensed, wait at the ready position until the incensing of the Celebrant is completed before approaching the altar.

When the Priest faces them, Server 1 and Server 2 make a simple bow. Server 1 carefully pours water over the fingers of the Priest while holding the bowl under the Priest's fingers.

After the Priest dries his hands, make a simple bow to the Priest, turn around, and return to the credence table. Put down all items and put the stoppers back on the cruets.

The Lavabo

Once Server 1 and Server 2 are done with the Lavabo, all altar servers walk in single file to their positions as seen in "7: Eucharistic Prayer (After Sanctus)" on page 52.

The Sanctus

Server 2 rings the sanctus bell. If the chasuble is to be raised at the Elevations, Server 1 joins the M.C. at the altar with the Priest. Both the M.C. and Server 1 stand a little behind the Priest on either side. All kneel at the conclusion of the *Sanctus*.

The Epiclesis

Normally, Server 2 rings the bells. Ring the bells once when the Priest extends his joined hands over the gifts (while praying the *epiclesis*).

The Consecration

If it is the custom at your parish, Server 1 and the M.C. may raise the Priest's chasuble at the Elevation of the Host, and again at the Elevation of the Chalice. Do not raise it too high!

Server 2 rings the bells at the Elevation of the Host, and again at the Elevation of the Chalice.

Following the Great Amen, all stand. If Server 1 has helped with the elevation of the chasuble, he returns to his place next to Server 2.

During Communion

After the Priest has taken his communion, all altar servers walk single file to the positions indicated in "8: Initial Server Communion Position" on page 52.

Server 1 (and Server 2 on Sundays and Solemnities) take up the communion patens.

Following Communion, the Communion patens are placed on the altar or the credence table with the other sacred vessels.

Walking with the Communion Paten

Ablutions

AAfter the distribution of Holy Communion to the assembled faithful, Server 1 and Server 2 approach the altar, Server 1 with the water cruet and Server 2 with hands in the "joined hands" position. Server 1 then pours the water over the Priest's fingers into the chalice, stopping when he nods his head or gives another signal.

Server 1 and Server 2 receive the Communion patens and the other sacred vessels and/or linens that are removed from the altar. They make a simple bow and continue to help clear the altar as needed.

Remember to move together at all times, shoulder to shoulder!

Recessional

At the start of the Prayer after Communion (or the Saint Michael Prayer if that is the custom at your parish), the Cross Bearer retrieves the processional Cross while Server 1 and Server 2 retrieve their candles.

At the start of the closing hymn, the Cross Bearer, Server 1, and Server 2 walk into the Nave. Go about three pews down the center aisle and then turn around to face the sanctuary. Make the appropriate reverence in unison with the Priest.

The Cross Bearer, Server 1, and Server 2 turn around and process shoulder to shoulder down the main aisle of the Nave.

After Mass

Server 1 and Server 2 extinguish the altar candles in the reverse order from which they had been lit.

The bell shaped extinguisher is used to snuff candles out without smashing down on the wick. The bell should be lowered enough only enough to cover the flame and suffocate it. Altar candles are *never* extinguished by blowing them out.

BOAT BEARER

The boat should be held cupped in your right hand, with your left hand over your heart.

The Boat Bearer should always walk next to the Thurifer, but perhaps a half-step behind so that you don't accidentally walk into the thurible when turning a corner. Stick with the Thurifer, and you won't go wrong.

Before Mass

Arrive 30 minutes before Mass, and complete these tasks within the first fifteen minutes:
- Sign in and be vested, having said the vesting prayers.
- Make sure that the boat is full. If it is not, tell the Thurifer or the M.C.

Entrance Procession

When the Priest Celebrant is ready, the Boat Bearer gives the boat to him (or to the Deacon or M.C. as instructed). When the imposing of incense is finished, the Boat Bearer receives the boat back.

Processing is always done solemnly, at a moderate pace, and with a distance of three pews between each group of altar servers.

If your parish is using "Option B: Lining Up at the Foot" on page 41: when you arrive at the foot of the altar, turn towards your left and line up as shown in "2: Arrival at the Foot of the Altar" on page 41.

After you genuflect or bow, proceed up the steps.

Introductory Rites

When Priest Celebrant is ready, the Boat Bearer gives the boat to him (or to the Deacon or M.C. as instructed).

The Celebrant incenses the Cross and the altar. Stand attentively with the boat in hand and wait for him to finish. When he hands the thurible back to the Thurifer, bow and walk back to the sacristy with the Thurifer and put the boat away.

Liturgy of the Word

Gospel Procession

At the beginning of the third antiphon of the Responsorial Psalm, the Thurifer, Boat Bearer, Server 1, Server 2, and two Candle Bearers rise from their seats and walk to the sacristy. Obtain the boat.

As the *Alleluia* or *verse before the Gospel* begins, follow the Thurifer to the Priest and wait a few steps short of the Presider's Chair. See "5a: The Four-Candle Procession (with Thurifer)" on page 45.

Once the Priest imposes the incense, proceed to the altar and take your position.

When the Priest or Deacon, having held up the *Book of the Gospels*, turns toward the Ambo, you likewise turn to face the Ambo, and all proceed as shown in "From the Altar to the Ambo" on page 49.

Candle Bearers take up their positions on either side of the Ambo. You take your position just behind the Priest or Deacon, next to the Thurifer. At the words "the Gospel of the Lord", respond "Praise to you, Lord Jesus Christ."

Then, turn towards the sacristy, and return there with the Thurifer. Remain with him until it is time to return to your seat and listen attentively to the remainder of the homily.

Liturgy of the Eucharist

Following the conclusion of the prayers of the faithful, while the other altar servers walk across the sanctuary, the Thurifer and the Boat Bearer walk to the sacristy to obtain the thurible and boat. Meet the other altar servers at the step near the credence table and wait for the Offertory.

Offertory

Stay next to the Thurifer and follow any instructions he gives you. Present the boat as instructed. Return with the Thurifer to the ambulatory to meet up with the Torchbearers.

Eucharistic Prayer

At the *Sanctus*, take your position with the Thurifer and Torchbearers at the foot of the altar, as indicated in "7: Eucharistic Prayer (After Sanctus)" on page 52. Upon reaching your place, at the signal from the Thurifer, kneel.

Following the Great Amen, stand and retire the boat to the sacristy.

During Communion

After the Priest has taken his communion, all altar servers walk single file to the positions indicated in "8: Initial Server Communion Position" on page 52.

After you take Communion, go and stand at your seat, unless instructed otherwise by the Thurifer, M.C., Deacon, or Priest.

Recessional

Go to the foot of the altar with the Thurifer. Turn, face the sanctuary, and wait for the Priest. Make the appropriate reverence in unison with the Priest.

After Mass

After the Blessing of the Servers, return to the sacristy.

Book Bearer

A liturgical book is held open in one of three ways:
1. An open (or closed) book may be held against the chest, with the top part of the book beneath the neck, and both hands under the bottom edge;
2. If the altar server is taller than the Priest, an open book may be held to the altar server's left side with the left hand on the bottom-left edge of the book, while the right hand holds the top right-hand corner of the book; or,
3. If the altar server is significantly shorter than the Priest, an open book is held against the forehead, with both hands under the bottom edge.

The Priest will let you know how he would like you to hold the book.

Before Mass

Arrive 30 minutes before Mass, and complete these tasks within the first fifteen minutes:
- Sign in and be vested, having said the vesting prayers.
- Unless the M.C. or Priest has done so, make sure that the ribbons for the *Missal* and any other ritual books are in the proper places.

Be prepared to do the following at the instruction of the M.C. or the Celebrant:
- Place the *Missal* on the Missal table.
- Place the Celebrant's binder at the Presider's table.

Entrance Procession

The Book Bearer should process with folded hands behind the Cross Bearer[1]. Processing is always done solemnly, at a moderate pace, and with a distance of three pews between each group of altar servers.

If your parish is using "Option B: Lining Up at the Foot" on page 41: when you arrive at the foot of the altar, turn towards your right/left and line up as shown in "2: Arrival at the Foot of the Altar" on page 41.

After you genuflect or bow, proceed up the steps.

Upon entering the sanctuary, stand at attention at your seat, prepared to assist the Priest during the Greeting and the Penitential Act if needed.

For the Collect, when we sing the "Amen" in the *Gloria*, present the *Missal* to the M.C. (or Server 1 if there is no M.C.) He will open it to the correct page. When the Priest says "Let us pray", bring the *Missal* to the Priest.

Hold the *Missal* open until the Priest says "Amen". Then close the *Missal* and return it to the assigned place.

---

1. If serving a Pontifical Mass, the Book Bearer walks in procession behind the Bishop he serves. The Priest or M.C. may ask you to process with a ritual book. See "Carrying a Book in Procession" on page 32.

Liturgy of the Word

After the Homily, stand ready to assist the Priest, if necessary, during the Creed and prayers of the faithful.

Liturgy of the Eucharist

Following the conclusion of the prayers of the faithful, take the missal stand[1] and accompany Server 1 and Server 2 to just behind the main altar. Bow. Place the *Missal*, return to your place in the triangle formation, and all bow to the altar together again.

Continue to the credence table.

While the altar is prepared, stand out of the way in the ready position.

Once Server 1 and Server 2 are done with the Lavabo, all altar servers walk in single file to their positions as seen in "7: Eucharistic Prayer (After Sanctus)" on page 52.

During Communion

After the Priest has taken his communion, all altar servers walk single file to the positions indicated in "8: Initial Server Communion Position" on page 52.

When the Priest, Servers, and any Deacons or Extraordinary Ministers have begun distributing Communion to the faithful, take *Missal* (and the Missal stand if applicable) from the altar to the missal table and stand at your seat.

Concluding Rites

Immediately upon standing, present the *Missal* to the M.C. He will open it to the correct page. When the Priest says "Let us pray", bring the *Missal* to the Priest. If there is a solemn blessing or a prayer over the people, be prepared to move at the Priest's instruction. At the Priest's signal or after the dismissal, close the *Missal* and return it to its assigned place.

Recessional

Proceed to the foot of the altar, taking the same position you took at the start of the Mass. Turn, face the sanctuary, and wait for the Priest. Make the appropriate reverence in unison with the Priest.

Turn and walk shoulder to shoulder with your partner (if any). See "9: Leaving the Sanctuary: the Recessional" on page 53 for more information.

After Mass

If required, bring the *Missal*, Presider's binder, and Lectionary back to the sacristy.

---

1. If instructed by the Priest or M.C., be prepared to bring the *Missal* without the stand to the altar instead.

CANDLE BEARER

Before Mass

Arrive 30 minutes before Mass, and complete these tasks within the first fifteen minutes:
- Sign in and be vested, having said the vesting prayers.

Entrance Procession

Processing is always done solemnly, at a moderate pace, and with a distance of three pews between each group of altar servers. The Candle Bearers walk ahead of the Deacon or Lector who is carrying the *Book of the Gospels* as an honor guard.

If your parish is using "Option B: Lining Up at the Foot" on page 41: when you arrive at the foot of the altar, turn towards your left and line up as shown in "2: Arrival at the Foot of the Altar" on page 41.

After you bow, proceed up the steps.

Walk to the sacristy as shown in "3: Preparing for the Introductory Rites" on page 42. Place your candles on the sacristy table and blow them out. Proceed to your seat and remain standing for the Introductory Rites.

Liturgy of the Word

Gospel Procession

At the beginning of the third antiphon of the Responsorial Psalm, the Thurifer, Boat Bearer, Server 1, Server 2, and the Candle Bearers rise from their seats and walk to the sacristy.

As the *Alleluia* or *verse before the Gospel* begins, follow the Thurifer to the Priest and wait a few steps short of the Presider's Chair. See "5a: The Four-Candle Procession (with Thurifer)" on page 45.

Once the Priest imposes the incense, proceed forward and wait for the Priest or Deacon to step in procession ahead of you. Then proceed to the altar and take your position.

When the Priest or Deacon, having held up the *Book of the Gospels*, turns toward the Ambo, you likewise turn to face the Ambo, and all proceed as shown in "From the Altar to the Ambo" on page 49.

Server 1, Server 2, and Candle Bearers take up their positions on either side of the Ambo while the Priest or Deacon proclaims the Gospel.

At the words "the Gospel of the Lord", respond "Praise to you, Lord Jesus Christ." Then, turn towards the sacristy, and return there, shoulder to shoulder, following the Thurifer if there is one. In the sacristy, extinguish your candles and return them to their place.

Return to your seats, all sitting at the same time, and listen attentively to the remainder of the homily.

DUTY SHEETS

Liturgy of the Eucharist

Offertory

If you are also serving as a Torchbearer: following the conclusion of the prayers of the faithful, while the other altar servers walk across the sanctuary, walk to the sacristy to obtain and light your torches. Once these are lit, go into the ambulatory and wait for the Thurifer.

If you are *not* serving as a Torchbearer: After being incensed by the Thurifer, turn and walk in single file to your positions as seen in "7: Eucharistic Prayer (After Sanctus)" on page 52.

Eucharistic Prayer

If you are also serving as a Torchbearer: at the *Sanctus*, take your position with the Thurifer and other Torchbearers at the foot of the altar, as indicated in "7: Eucharistic Prayer (After Sanctus)" on page 52. Upon reaching your place, at the signal from the Thurifer, kneel.

At both major elevations, salute the Precious Body / Precious Blood with your torch. Likewise, when the Priest genuflects, salute the Precious Body / Precious Blood with your torch.

Following the Great Amen, stand and take your positions as shown in "8: Initial Server Communion Position" on page 52.

Communion

If you are also serving as a Torchbearer: Remain in position until the tabernacle door is shut and the Priest and Servers have genuflected. Retire to the sacristy, extinguish your torches, and then return to stand at your seats.

If you are *not* serving as a Torchbearer: After the Priest has taken his communion, all altar servers walk single file to the positions indicated in "8: Initial Server Communion Position" on page 52.

After the Priest and Server 1 and Server 2 have walked to the foot of the altar to distribute Communion to the faithful, return to stand at your seats.

Recessional

Proceed to the foot of the altar. Turn, face the sanctuary, and wait for the Priest. Make the appropriate reverence in unison with the Priest. You will not carry candles or torches.

Turn and walk shoulder to shoulder. See "9: Leaving the Sanctuary: the Recessional" for more information.

After Mass

After the Blessing of the Servers, return to the sacristy.

CROSS BEARER

Sometimes known as the *Crucifer*, the Cross Bearer carries the processional Cross during the Entrance Procession, during the Offertory Procession, and at the end of Mass. If there is no Book Bearer, the Cross Bearer does this job in addition to his own.

You must be careful not to hit low hanging objects (lights, doorways, etc.) with the Cross. To avoid this, hold the Cross at an angle when walking through these areas. Where there is enough room, you should hold the Cross in this manner:

1. Hold the right hand about a foot above the left hand. This is the best way to hold the Cross balanced, without tipping over.
2. Hold the Cross straight up and down, with the corpus facing the front.
3. Don't hold the Cross too close to your body, but a little in front of it.
4. The corpus on the staff should be about two to three feet above your head when being carried.

Before Mass

Arrive 30 minutes before Mass, and complete these tasks within the first fifteen minutes:

- Sign in and be vested, having said the vesting prayers.
- Have the processional Cross ready in the sacristy.

Entrance Procession

If there is a Thurifer, you follow behind him. Otherwise, you lead the procession, flanked by Server 1 and Server 2.

Processing is always done solemnly, at a moderate pace, and with a distance of three pews between each group of altar servers.

If your parish is using "Option B: Lining Up at the Foot" on page 41: when you arrive at the foot of the altar, turn towards your right and line up as shown in "2: Arrival at the Foot of the Altar" on page 41.

After you bow, proceed up the steps with the Cross Bearer as shown in "3: Preparing for the Introductory Rites" on page 42. Repose the processional Cross in its place. All altar servers walk to their seats. Remain standing for the Introductory Rites.

Liturgy of the Eucharist

Following the conclusion of the prayers of the faithful, fetch the processional Cross for the Offertory procession. Go down the side aisle to the back of the nave. Once the collection is complete and those bearing the gifts are ready, lead them up the center aisle to the waiting Priest or Deacon. When you arrive, turn to your right and then to the foot of the altar. Bow to the altar and then proceed into the sanctuary. Repose the processional Cross in its place, and then return to stand at your seat.

Once Server 1 and Server 2 are done with the Lavabo, all altar servers walk in single file to their positions as seen in "7: Eucharistic Prayer (After Sanctus)" on page 52.

During Communion

After the Priest has taken his communion, all altar servers walk single file to the positions indicated in "8: Initial Server Communion Position" on page 52.

After you take Communion, you may be asked to stand watch (see "Standing Watch" on page 56). If not, go and stand at your seat unless instructed otherwise by the M.C., Deacon, or Priest.

Recessional

At the start of the Prayer after Communion (or the Saint Michael Prayer if that is the custom at your parish), the Cross Bearer retrieves the processional Cross while Server 1 and Server 2 retrieve their candles.

At the start of the closing hymn, the Cross Bearer, Server 1, and Server 2 walk into the Nave. Go about three pews down the center aisle and then turn around to face the sanctuary. Make the appropriate reverence in unison with the Priest.

The Cross Bearer, Server 1, and Server 2 turn around and process shoulder to shoulder down the main aisle of the Nave.

After Mass

After the Blessing of the Servers, the processional Cross is placed on the stand with the *corpus* facing out. The Cross Bearer divests and returns the vestments to their assigned place.

THURIFER

NOTE: The job of Thurifer is normally reserved to a Senior or Master Server if possible. They are the M.C.'s chief assistant, and they supervise the Boat Bearer and Torchbearers directly.

While processing with the thurible, you should:
- swing the thurible gently,
- do not allow the thurible to swing higher than the height of your waist,
- take care to walk solemnly and in the center of the aisle,
- take precautions when walking around corners, and
- do not swing the thurible when ascending or descending steps.

When holding the thurible but not walking, you should:
- Keep the cover slightly open (this will allow for an airflow and keep the cover cool) by holding the disk under the index finger and thumb of a clenched hand (but in a way that the chains are not crimped) and the cover chain ring draped over the disk and held by the thumb (or any other finger).
- When the office of the thurible is being exercised (i.e., when incense has been imposed and blessed), hold the thurible in the right hand; these times occur during:
  a. Processional,
  b. Gospel action, and
  c. Offertory incensations.
- Otherwise, when not exercising the office, hold the thurible in the left hand.

NOTE: If there is a Boat Bearer, their job is to assist you with the boat—let them do their job! Often this job is given to younger apprentices, so be gentle in guiding them in their duties. This job may also be given to more senior servers who are just learning to be a Thurifer. Be sure to set a good example.

Before Mass

Arrive 30 minutes before Mass, and complete these tasks within the first fifteen minutes:
- Sign in and be vested, having said the vesting prayers.
- Prepare charcoals and thurible items, making sure that the boat is full.

Fifteen minutes before the start of Mass, light the coals and place them in the thurible.

Entrance Procession

When Celebrant is ready, the Thurifer gives the boat to him (or to Deacon or M.C. as instructed) and opens the thurible for the imposition of incense. When the imposing of incense is finished, the Thurifer receives the boat back and then takes his place at the head of the formation of altar servers to lead the procession.

Processing is always done solemnly, at a moderate pace, and with a distance of three pews between each group of altar servers.

Altar Server Duties

If your parish is using "Option B: Lining Up at the Foot" on page 41: when you arrive at the foot of the altar, turn towards your left and line up as shown in "2: Arrival at the Foot of the Altar" on page 41.

After you genuflect or bow, proceed up the steps and stand ready as shown in "3: Preparing for the Introductory Rites" on page 42.

Introductory Rites

When the Priest Celebrant is ready, the Thurifer gives the boat to him (or Deacon or M.C. as instructed) and opens the thurible for the imposition of incense.

The Celebrant incenses the Cross and the altar. Stand attentively with the boat in hand and wait for the Celebrant to finish. When he hands the thurible back to you, bow and walk back to the sacristy with the thurible and boat and put them where they go.

Liturgy of the Word

Gospel Procession

At the beginning of the third antiphon of the Responsorial Psalm, the Thurifer, Boat Bearer, Server 1, Server 2, and two Candle Bearers rise from their seats and walk to the sacristy.

Obtain the thurible (and boat if there is no Boat Bearer).

As the *Alleluia* or *verse before the Gospel* begins, the Thurifer (with Boat Bearer) leads the procession and goes to the Priest. See "5a: The Four-Candle Procession (with Thurifer)" on page 45.

Once the Priest imposes the incense, proceed to the altar and take your position.

When the Priest or Deacon, having held up the *Book of the Gospels*, turns toward the Ambo, you likewise turn to face the Ambo, and all proceed as shown in "From the Altar to the Ambo" on page 49.

Candle Bearers take up their positions on either side of the Ambo. You take your position behind the Priest or Deacon.

After the Priest or Deacon incenses the Gospel, remain in place gently swinging the thurible, while the Gospel is proclaimed. At the words "the Gospel of the Lord", respond "Praise to you, Lord Jesus Christ."

Then, turn towards the sacristy, and return there, leading Server 1, Server 2, and the two Candle Bearers. In the sacristy, return the thurible to its place. Prepare an additional coal if necessary for the Liturgy of the Eucharist. Keep the Boat Bearer with you.

Return to your seat and listen attentively to the remainder of the homily.

Liturgy of the Eucharist

Following the conclusion of the prayers of the faithful, while the other altar servers walk across the sanctuary, the Thurifer walks to the sacristy to obtain the thurible and boat. Meet the other altar servers near the credence table and wait for the Offertory.

Offertory

NOTE: If there is a Deacon, he will do much of the next steps. Take your cue from him.

When the Celebrant is ready, the Thurifer gives the boat to him (or Deacon or M.C.) and opens the thurible for the imposition of incense. The Celebrant incenses the altar. Repose the Boat at the Ambo and then stand attentively and wait for the Celebrant to finish. When he hands the thurible back to you, bow and incense him.

If there are additional clerics, incense them next.

Then proceed to the center of the sanctuary at the top of the steps and turn to incense the M.C. with a single swing. From this position, turn to incense the altar servers who are not engaged in other tasks.

Then incense the people. Following this, return to the sacristy with the Torchbearers.

Eucharistic Prayer

At the *Sanctus*, take your position with the Thurifer and Torchbearers at the foot of the altar, as indicated in "7: Eucharistic Prayer (After Sanctus)" on page 52. When the Torchbearers are in place, make a signal and kneel.

At both major elevations, incense the Precious Body / Precious Blood.

Following the Great Amen, stand and retire the thurible to the sacristy.

During Communion

After the Priest has taken his communion, all altar servers walk single file to the positions indicated in "8: Initial Server Communion Position" on page 52.

After you take Communion, you may be asked to stand watch (see "Standing Watch" on page 56). If you are not, go and stand at your seat unless instructed otherwise by the M.C., Deacon, or Priest.

Recessional

Proceed to the foot of the altar. Turn, face the sanctuary, and wait for the Priest. Make the appropriate reverence in unison with the Priest.

After Mass

After the Blessing of the Servers, return to the sacristy. Dump out the thurible into the appropriate receptacle.

Altar Server Duties

Torchbearer

Before Mass

Arrive 30 minutes before Mass, and complete these tasks within the first fifteen minutes:
- Sign in and be vested, having said the vesting prayers.
- If the M.C. indicates that torches will be used in the Entrance Procession, at five minutes before Mass is to begin, obtain and light your torch.

Entrance Procession

Processing is always done solemnly, at a moderate pace, and with a distance of three pews between each group of altar servers.

If your parish is using "Option B: Lining Up at the Foot" on page 41: when you arrive at the foot of the altar, turn towards your right or left as appropriate and line up as shown in "2: Arrival at the Foot of the Altar" on page 41. Note that you will be separating from your partner when you do this. After you bow, wait for all other altar servers to pass you before you proceed up the steps in single file as shown in "3: Preparing for the Introductory Rites" on page 42.

Otherwise, after you bow proceed up the steps.

Go to the sacristy to retire and extinguish your torches. Then, proceed to your seat and remain standing for the Introductory Rites.

Thurifer, Boat Bearer, and Torchbearers during the Eucharistic Prayer

Liturgy of the Word

Listen attentively to the readings, saying the usual responses. Sing the Responsorial Psalm. Stand for the Gospel as normal. Listen attentively to the homily.

Liturgy of the Eucharist

Offertory

Following the conclusion of the prayers of the faithful, while the other altar servers walk across the sanctuary, walk to the sacristy to obtain and light your torch. Once these are lit, go into the ambulatory and wait for the Thurifer. Follow the instructions of the Thurifer.

Eucharistic Prayer

At the *Sanctus*, take your position with the Thurifer at the foot of the altar, as indicated in "7: Eucharistic Prayer (After Sanctus)" on page 52. Upon reaching your place, at the signal from the Thurifer, kneel.

At both major elevations, salute the Precious Body / Precious Blood with your torch.

When the Priest genuflects, salute the Precious Body / Precious Blood with your torch.

Following the Great Amen, stand and take your positions as shown in "8: Initial Server Communion Position" on page 52.

The Torchbearers Salute

Communion

Remain in position until the tabernacle is shut and the Priest and Servers have genuflected. Retire to the sacristy, extinguish your torches, and then return to stand at your seats.

Recessional

Proceed to the foot of the altar. Turn, face the sanctuary, and wait for the Priest. Make the appropriate reverence in unison with the Priest.

Turn and walk shoulder to shoulder in pairs. See "9: Leaving the Sanctuary: the Recessional" on page 53 for more information.

After Mass

After the Blessing of the Servers, return to the sacristy.

CROZIER BEARER / MITER BEARER

In Masses with a Bishop (a "Pontifical Mass"), there will be a Crozier Bearer (Crb) and a Miter Bearer (Mib). Together, these are sometimes called "vimps" for their unique vesture: the vimpa.

Before Mass

Arrive 30 minutes before Mass, and complete these tasks within the first fifteen minutes:
- Sign in and be vested, having said the vesting prayers.
- Make sure your vimpa is placed correctly over the surplice or alb and tied securely.
- Find the M.C. and follow any additional instructions they may give you.

When the M.C. gives the signal, as a pair, walk through the ambulatory to the Priest's sacristy. Here you will be introduced to the Bishop and be given any last minute instructions. From this point on, you will follow the Bishop.

Procession

Processing is always done solemnly and at a moderate pace. The Crb and MiB walk one pew-length behind the Bishop, slightly flanking him, as in the Triangle formation.

When you arrive at the final pew before the foot of the altar, stop and back-sweep towards the pew on the south side. The M.C. will hand you the Bishop's miter and crozier. Sweep back into the aisle and bow before proceeding up the steps to your seats.

During the Mass

You will not really leave the vicinity of your seats during the Mass. You will even take your Communion there! The M.C. will signal you whenever you need to present or take the miter or crozier. When you are signalled, both stand at the same time and approach the M.C. He will take items from the Bishop and give them to you, or take items from you to present to the Bishop, or both. Whenever this transaction is complete, return to your seats.

Recessional

After the Bishop makes his reverence to the altar, at the signal from the M.C., proceed to the foot of the altar. Turn, face the sanctuary, and make the appropriate reverence. Turn around and walk shoulder to shoulder, following behind the Bishop as you did in the entrance procession.

After Mass

After the Blessing of the Servers, remain with the Bishop until he dismisses you. Then return to the sacristy to divest.

DUTY SHEETS

MASTER OF CEREMONIES

The Master of Ceremonies (M.C.) is not an altar server. He does, however, direct the altar servers and, at times, in addition to his own duties, may perform the duties of an altar server. He must know how to perform not only his own job, but also those of everyone else. He must also know how to correct a ceremonial situation with discretion.

Before Mass
- Arrive at least 30 minutes before the start of Mass.
- Vest in cassock and surplice[1] or in alb and cincture as appropriate while praying the appropriate prayers.
- Consult with the Priest regarding any special notes for this Mass.
- Check the *Roman Missal*, making sure that it is marked correctly.
- Confirm that the appropriate vessels and vestments (and microphone!) are set out in their assigned places.
- Direct all preparations, ensuring that altar servers remain silent and that their duties are completed in a timely and orderly manner.
- If one or more of the assigned altar servers has not arrived by fifteen (15) minutes before the start of Mass, reassign their scheduled duties as appropriate.
- If called upon, assist the Celebrant in vesting.

Procession

In the sacristy, the M.C. supervises the formation of the procession. The M.C. faces the processional Cross, signals all to bow towards it, and leads the prayer (see "Prayer of the Servers Before Leaving the Sacristy" on page 4).

When the procession reaches the narthex, the M.C. supervises the altar servers as they await the Priest for the prayers before Mass. Afterwards, he leads the procession into the nave and ensures that all pairs are spaced about three pews apart.

If there is to be incense in the entrance procession, the M.C. may assist with the incense. He receives the boat and hands it to the Priest. Then, he receives the thurible from the Thurifer and holds it open for the Priest, who places incense on the lit charcoal and blesses it. The M.C. returns the boat and the thurible to the Thurifer.

The M.C.'s customary place in the procession is behind the Lector(s)[2]. At his discretion, however, and keeping in mind the relative solemnity of the occasion, he may pair with the Book Bearer instead.

---

1. However, the custom of the M.C. "putting on the surplice only directly before Mass seems praiseworthy". Fortescue, p. 121.
2. See Elliott, *Ceremonies of the Modern Roman Rite*, no. 376 and diagram 2. If, however, a Deacon carries the *Book of the Gospels*, the M.C. walks *in front* of him and his Candle Bearers instead. In most cases, this means pairing the M.C. with the Book Bearer regardless.

Introductory Rites

If your parish is using "Option B: Lining Up at the Foot" on page 41, the M.C. stops at the Foot with the Priest and the altar servers. All make the appropriate reverence. The Priest approaches the altar.

After the Priest reverences the altar with a kiss, the M.C. may assist the Priest with the incensation of the altar. The M.C. approaches the side of the altar, faces the Thurifer, receives the boat, and hands it to the Priest. Then he faces the Thurifer, receives the thurible, and presents it open to the Priest. After the Priest makes a sign of the Cross over the incensed charcoal, the M.C. closes the thurible, receives the boat, hands the thurible to the Priest, and returns the boat to the Thurifer.

The M.C. attends the Priest as the altar is incensed. When the incensation has been completed, the M.C. receives the thurible from the Priest and returns it to the Thurifer.

Liturgy of the Word

Gospel Procession

At the beginning of the third antiphon of the Responsorial Psalm, the M.C. and the appropriate altar servers rise from their seats and walk to the sacristy. The M.C. may wish to subtly signal them to stand, so that everyone stands at the same time.

As the *Alleluia* or *verse before the Gospel* begins, follow at the end of the procession, unless called upon by the Priest to assist with the imposition of incense, in which case walk behind the Thurifer (and Boat). Then proceed to the altar and take your position.

When the Priest or Deacon, having held up the *Book of the Gospels*, turns toward the Ambo, you likewise turn to face the Ambo, and all proceed as shown in the diagram ""4: Seating" on page 44. Take up the proper position next to the Thurifer while the Priest or Deacon proclaims the Gospel.

The M.C. may be called upon to assist with the incensation of the Gospel. Before the proclamation of the Gospel, the M.C. receives the thurible from the Thurifer and hands it to the Priest or Deacon. After the incensation, the Priest or Deacon hands the thurible back to the M.C., who returns it to the Thurifer.

At the words "the Gospel of the Lord", respond "Praise to you, Lord Jesus Christ".

If it is the custom at your parish, stand next to the credence table while the altar servers return to the sacristy, and when the Priest or Deacon hands you the Book of the Gospels, take it around the front of the ambo and place it in its seat.

Return to the sacristy and lead the altar servers in returning to their places.

Liturgy of the Eucharist

At the conclusion of the Prayer of the Faithful, the M.C. may be called upon by the Priest to arrange the altar.

The M.C. approaches the altar and sets the altar as follows: He receives the chalice from the servers and places it on the right side of the altar. He unfolds the corporal, centering it on the altar. The corporal should not be turned over. It is left with the creases down.

The chalice is placed on the corporal to the rear leaving room for the paten. The chalice veil and burse are returned to the credence table by Server 1. The pall is removed and set to the right of the corporal. The M.C. receives any additional vessels or linens and arranges them according to the usual arrangement.

The M.C. Assists the Priest with the Missal

Offertory

At the Offertory Procession, the M.C. may join the Priest and the altar servers at the Foot.

After the gifts have been accepted, the M.C. returns to the left and rear of the Priest to assist with the *Missal*.

When the altar is incensed, the M.C. may be called upon to assist.

Eucharistic Prayer

The M.C. remains at the altar. The M.C. and Server 1 kneel following the *Sanctus*. If it is the custom at your parish, they may raise and lower the chasuble as the Priest raises and lowers the Host. They bow when the Priest genuflects. They do the same when the Priest raises and lowers the chalice. They bow when the Priest genuflects. They stand at the Great Amen.

If the chalice remains on the altar during the distribution of Holy Communion, the M.C. covers the chalice with the pall and after the end of Holy Communion, he uncovers it in preparation for the purification of the vessels.

Duties Following Mass

In the sacristy after Mass, the M.C. makes any corrections that are necessary in an encouraging manner. He supervises the altar servers as they perform their post-Mass duties and dismisses them after all duties are completed.

How to Serve Daily Mass

Typically, there is only one altar server at a daily Mass. This means you have to do the work of Server 1 and 2, *and* the Book Bearer, sometimes all at once. If there are two altar servers, they can split up the duties, with one doing the job of Server 1, and the other being both Server 2 and Book Bearer.

Before Mass

Arrive at least 15 minutes before Mass, and complete these tasks immediately:
- Sign in and vest, having said the vesting prayers.
- Make sure that the ribbons for the *Missal* are in the proper places. For most daily Masses that aren't a Memorial or Feast, at least one ribbon should be for the previous Sunday Mass and one should be for the Preface. Consult with the Sacristan if you are unsure how to read the *Ordo* or set the *Missal*.
- Place the *Missal* on the missal stand.
- Make sure the Priest's microphone has fresh batteries.
- At ten minutes before the Mass is to begin, light the candles (see "Progressive Solemnity" on page 11 for the number of candles to light).

Procession

Process in front of the Priest from the Priest's sacristy. If your parish has a high altar with a tabernacle, face it and at the Priest's signal, genuflect. Otherwise, face the main altar and bow with the Priest. Proceed to your seat and remain standing for the Introductory Rites, prepared to assist the Priest during the Greeting and the Penitential Act if needed.

When the Priest says "Let us pray", bring the *Missal* to him, open to the correct page if possible.

Hold the *Missal* open until the Priest says "Amen". Then close the *Missal* and return it to the assigned place.

Liturgy of the Word

After the Homily, stand ready to assist the Priest, if necessary, during the prayers of the faithful.

Gospel Procession (for a single server)

At the *beginning* of the Responsorial Psalm, rise from your seat and walk to the sacristy. Light a single processional candle.

As the *Alleluia* or *verse before the Gospel* begins, enter the sanctuary and proceed to the side of the ambo. Take up your position there while the Priest proclaims the Gospel.

At the words "the Gospel of the Lord", respond "Praise to you, Lord Jesus Christ." Then, turn towards the sacristy, and return there. In the sacristy, extinguish your candle.

Return to your seat and listen attentively to the remainder of the homily.

Liturgy of the Eucharist

Following the conclusion of the prayers of the faithful, take the missal stand to just behind the main altar. Bow. Place the missal stand and bow to the altar again before proceeding to the credence table.

Offertory

Bring the vested chalice assembly to the altar. Place the items reverently on the altar in their proper place. After the altar has been arranged, stand in the ready position with the unstoppered water cruet in hand. When the Priest indicates, proceed to the side of the altar.

When the Priest faces you, make a simple bow and present the water cruet. When you receive it back, make a simple bow and return to the credence table. Prepare the lavabo items as soon as you return to the credence table.

NOTE: If serving solo and there are two cruets, one for water and one for wine, hold the wine cruet in your right hand and the water cruet in your left hand. Make a simple bow and present the wine cruet to the Priest, immediately transferring the water cruet from your left hand to your right hand. Then receive the wine cruet into your left hand and present the water cruet to the Priest with your right hand, transferring the wine cruet from your left hand to your right hand as before. Receive the water cruet into your left hand, and then make a simple bow, returning the cruets to the credence table. This sounds complicated, but with a little practice, you will soon be doing this naturally and easily.

Lavabo

Facing the credence table, pick up the lavabo bowl and the water cruet. Keep the water cruet in the right hand, drape the towel over your left arm, and pick up the lavabo bowl with the left hand.

Approach the side of the altar. When the Priest faces you, make a simple bow. Carefully pour water over the fingers of the Priest while holding the bowl under the Priest's fingers.

After the Priest dries his hands, make a simple bow to the Priest and return to the credence table. Put down all items and put the stoppers back on the cruets.

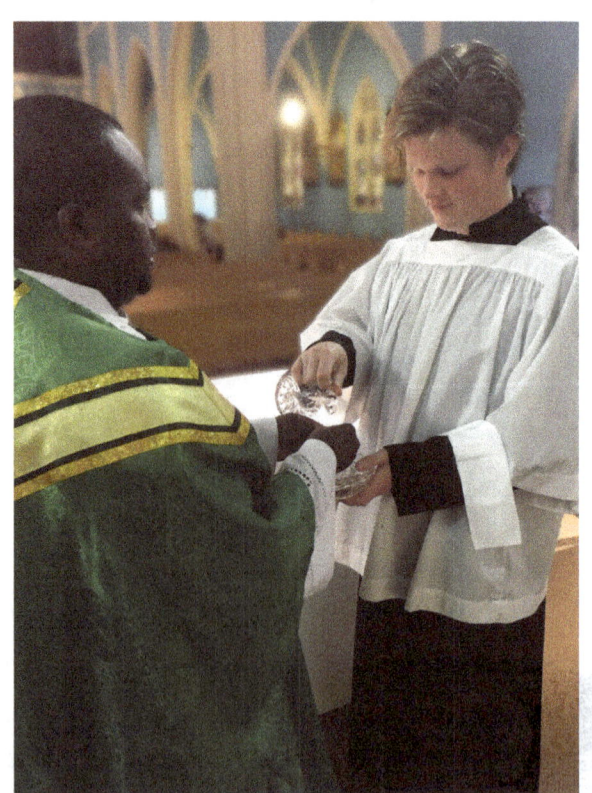

Once you are done with the Lavabo, walk to the Server 2 position as seen in "7: Eucharistic Prayer (After Sanctus)" on page 52.

The Sanctus

Ring the sanctus bell at the appropriate time. If the raising of the chasuble is the custom at your parish, after saying the words *Benedictus qui venint in nomine Domini* ("Blessed is he who comes in the name of the Lord"), *quietly* carry the altar bells and take up to the Server 1 spot slightly behind the Priest and to his right. Kneel at the conclusion of the *Sanctus*. Keep the bells in hand.

The Epiclesis

Ring the bells once when the Priest extends his joined hands over the gifts (while praying the *epiclesis*).

The Consecration

If it is the custom at your parish, raise the Priest's chasuble at the Elevation of the Host. At the same time, ring the bells. Bow when the Priest genuflects. Repeat the procedure at the Elevation of the chalice, setting down the bells as you bow this time.

Following the Great Amen, take the bells and stand. Return to the Server 2 position.

The Sign of Peace

After you have received the Sign of Peace from the Priest, if it is the custom at your parish, place a kneeler in the place where the Priest will distribute Communion, so that those people who wish to receive Communion keeling may more easily do so. Return to you place when you have done this.

During Communion

After the Priest has taken his Communion, walk to the credence table and take the Communion paten. Receive and then assist the Priest with Communion.

Following Communion, place the Communion paten on the altar.

Ablutions

After the distribution of Holy Communion to the assembled faithful, bring the water cruet to the altar. Pour the water over the Priest's fingers into the chalice, stopping when he nods his head or gives another signal. Wait for him to purify the Communion paten, then make a simple bow and take the cruet and the Communion paten back to the credence table.

Bring the chalice veil and burse to the Priest and receive from him the reassembled chalice assembly. Bow and return it to the credence table.

On your way back to your seat, take the missal stand from the altar exactly in the same way you first put it there and return it to its assigned place.

Concluding Rites

When the Priest says, "Let us pray", bring the *Missal* to the Priest. If there is a solemn blessing or a prayer over the people, be prepared to move at the Priest's instruction. After the Dismissal, close the *Missal* and return it to its assigned place.

Recessional

Following any announcements (and the Prayer to Saint Michael if this is the custom at your parish), proceed to the high altar, taking your position at the Priest's right (so you can lead him out). Make the appropriate reverence in unison with the Priest.

Turn and walk back to the Priest's vesting sacristy. Father will bless you in the sacristy.

After Mass

- Extinguish the altar candles.
- Bring the *Missal* back to the sacristy.
- Bring the kneeler (if used) back to its place.

Altar Server Duties

GLOSSARY

THE CHURCH

The map below uses a liturgical compass. When the faithful in the Nave face the Altar, they face *Liturgical East*, where the sun rises and the day begins, representing the Resurrection and a new creation.

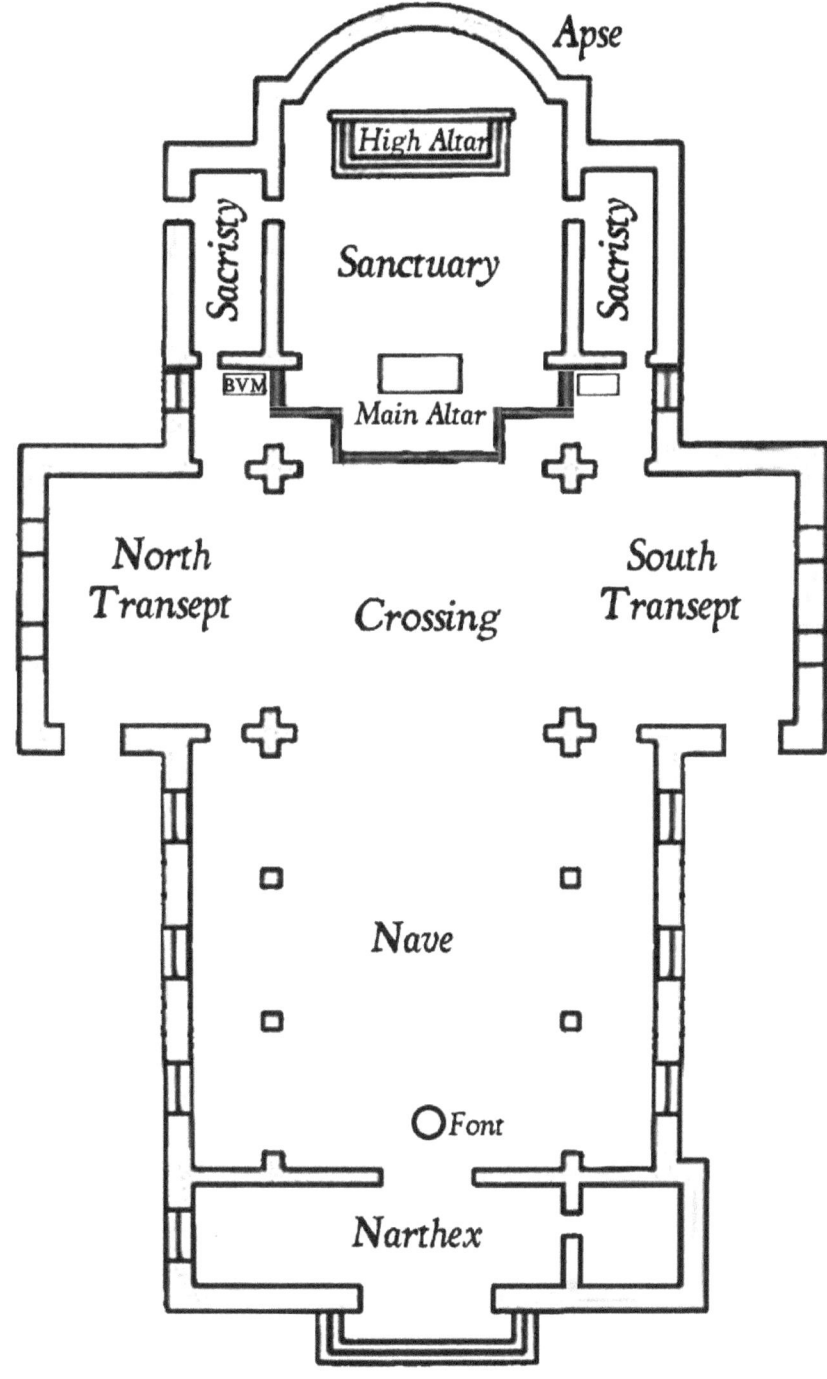

A Catholic Church Ground Floor Plan

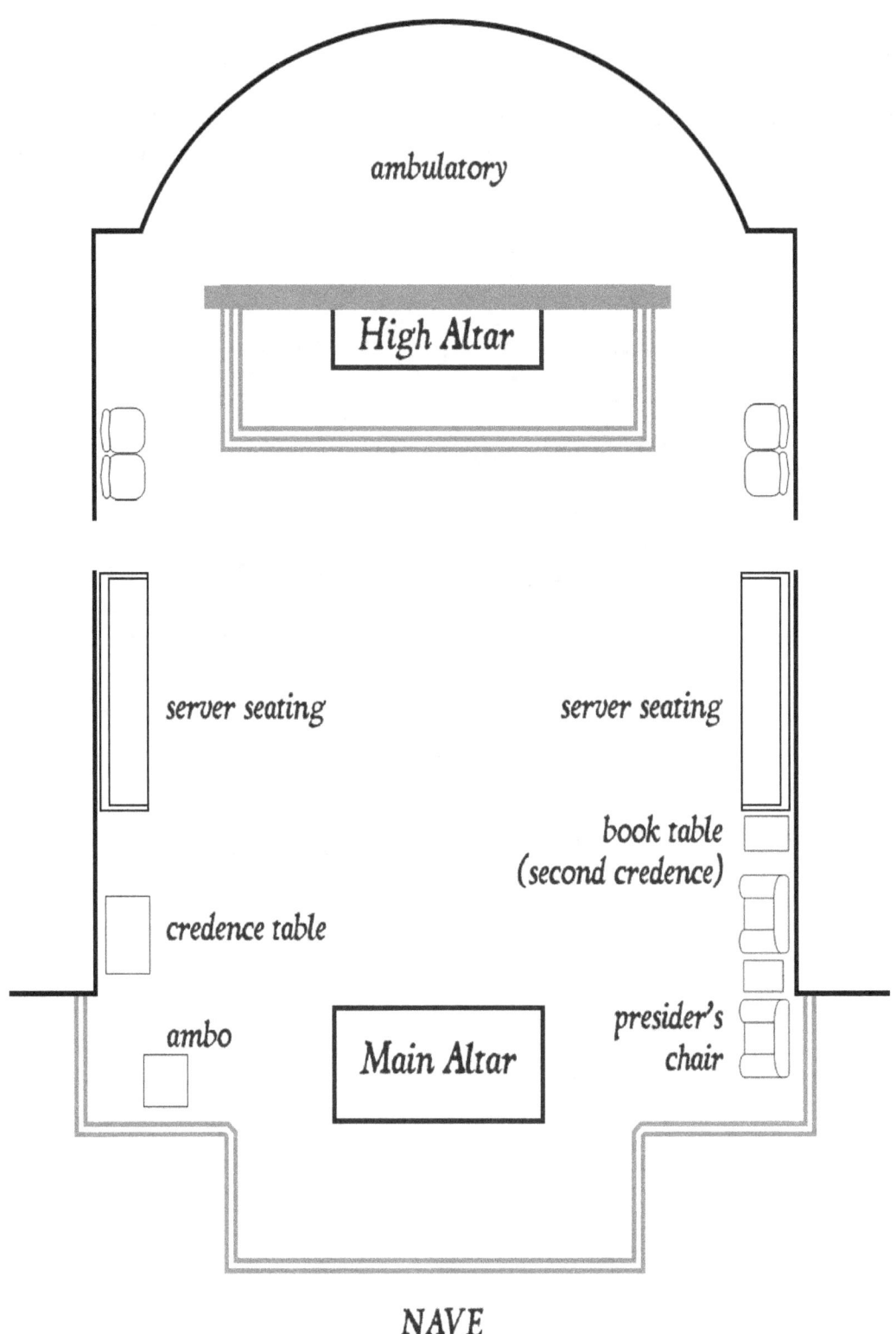

Altar and Sanctuary Furnishings

1. High Altar
2. Altar Cross
3. Credence Table
4. Candlestick
5. Tabernacle
6. Tabernacle Veil
7. Gradines -or- Shelves of the Altar
8. Sanctuary Lamp
9. Mensa -or- Table of the Altar
10. Predella -or- Platform of the Altar
11. Antependium
12. Main Altar
13. Ambo
14. Presider's Table
15. Presider's Chair

SACRED SPACE: DEFINITIONS

Altar The Altar of Sacrifice is the *mensa* (table) on which the one bloody sacrifice of Calvary is offered in an unbloody manner and the Body and Blood of our Lord is made present. It often sits on a platform called the *predella*.

Ambo The platform, lectern, or pulpit from which the Word of God is proclaimed and the homily is given.

Ambry A receptacle that houses the holy oils (Oil of the Sick, Oil of Catechumens, and the Sacred Chrism). The word Ambry is derived from the Latin word *armarium*, which means "closet."

Ambulatory

> The ambulatory is a walkway behind the high altar. The word ambulatory is derived from the Latin word *ambulo*, which means "I walk."

Apse   The apse is the architectural structure which surrounds the rear of the sanctuary. The word apse derives from the Latin word *apsis*, which means "arch or vault."

Baptismal Font

> The stone bowl often found either near the sanctuary or in the passageway from the narthex to the nave that is used for the Sacrament of Baptism.

Credence Table

> The table (or tables) in the sanctuary where the cruets, chalices, and ciboria are kept before and after the Consecration.

Font   See *Baptismal Font*.

Foot of the Altar

> The ground just before the first step of the predella of the altar.

Narthex   The area of the church near the entrance but outside the nave. When in the narthex, the faithful are not yet technically inside the church. In the early Church, penitents and catechumens (unbaptized persons preparing for Baptism) were confined to this area until their reconciliation with or admittance into the Church took place.

Nave   The nave is the area where the faithful assemble: it's where the pews are. From the Latin word for ship, *navis*, with the idea that the assembled faithful are on a ship that keeps them safe on their journey to Heaven.

Paschal Candle

> The paschal candle symbolizes Jesus Christ crucified. At the Easter Vigil, five grains of incense, symbolizing the Five Wounds of Christ, are inserted into the paschal candle in the form of a Cross. It is made of beeswax, which symbolizes the pure flesh of Christ. The wick signifies the soul of Christ. The flame represents His divinity. All candles used in liturgical functions are to be seen as extensions of the paschal candle. The word paschal comes from the Latin word *pasch*, which comes from the Hebrew word *pesach*, which means "Passover." The Paschal Candle is only lit during the Easter Season and at Baptisms and funerals.

Predella   The platform on which an altar is usually placed. It often has a number of steps, traditionally three.

Presider's Chair

> The seat of the Celebrating Priest at Mass. Additional nearby seats may be set up for any concelebrating Priest(s) and / or Deacon(s). See also *Sedilia*.

Prie-dieu

> A small, ornamental wooden desk furnished with a thin, sloping shelf for books or hands, and a kneeler. It comes from the French meaning "pray to God". Sometimes called a kneeler.

Reliquary / Sepulcrum

> The cavity on the altar in which the relic(s) of the patron saints of that church or chapel are incased.

Sacrarium

> A sink with its drain going directly into the earth, usually fitted with a cover and lock which is used for the disposal of the following:
> - sacred linen wash and rinse water,
> - used holy water,
> - used baptismal water,
> - holy oils,
> - blessed ashes.
>
> No other use is allowed. It is usually located in the working sacristy.

Sacristy The room where the Priest, sacristans, and other ministers prepare for the celebration of Mass. Larger churches may have more than one, typically a working sacristy and a Priestly vesting sacristy. The sacristy is the area where the sacred vestments, vessels, and linens are stored. The words sacristy and sacrarium are both derived from the Latin word *Sacer*, which means "sacred."

Sanctuary

> The sanctuary is the holy place where the ordained celebrate the sacred mysteries. The word sanctuary is derived from the Latin word *sanctus*, which means "holy." Aside from being the place of the Altar, the sanctuary is also the place where the tabernacle is usually kept. A sanctuary lamp is kept lit to indicate and honor the presence of the Eucharistic Christ in the tabernacle.

Sedilia (Plural. Singular form is *sedile*) Originally, stone seats found on the south side of an altar for the use by the Priest and his assistants, the Deacon and Subdeacon. No longer used in the modern Roman Rite, though older churches may still have them. See *Presider's Chair*.

Stoup Holy water fountain or bowl at the entrances of the church. There are also traditionally stoups in sacristies for use when entering the nave or sanctuary.

Amice The amice is used, if necessary, to cover street clothing[1] when wearing an alb. A Priest puts it on his head first, recalling when Jesus was blindfolded and mocked, as well as when he was crowned with thorns. The Priest then places it on his shoulders. The word amice comes from the Latin word *amictus*, which means "mantle."

Alb A long, white tunic-like garment that reaches from the neck to the heels, usually tied by a cincture. The alb is a symbol of baptism, reminiscent of the baptismal garment. The word alb comes from the Latin word *albus*, which means "white."

Cassock A long, black tunic-like garment that reaches from the neck to the heels. It is worn by some servers and clergy. Cardinals may wear one of red color or with red piping, cincture, and buttons; a bishop may wear purple. The Pope's is always white. Many cassocks have thirty-three buttons, symbolizing the years of the life of Jesus. The word, cassock, comes from the Italian word *casacca*, which means "long coat." Sometimes called a *soutane*.

Chasuble

Priestly vestment for Mass. The chasuble recalls the purple cloth that Pilate's soldiers put upon Christ in mockery, declaring him King of the Jews. The word chasuble comes from the Latin word *casupula*, which means "little house." The vestment is called this because it covers everything else.

Cincture A belt, girdle, or cord tied around the waist of an alb. It sometimes has a tassel of the liturgical color of the day. It symbolizes chastity. The word cincture comes from the Latin word *cinctus*, which means "to gird."

Cope A large semi-circular cloak, reaching to the feet and having a small cape in the back. It is clasped in front at the breast. The cope is worn by the officiating Priest at Benediction of the Blessed Sacrament and in processions. It is also sometimes used in solemn blessings such as the blessing of the palms on Palm Sunday. The word cope comes from the Latin word *cappa*, meaning "cloak."

Crozier The crozier is the shepherd's staff used by Bishops. It is a symbol of the Bishop's pastoral role. The word crozier derives from the German word *crosse*, which means "hooked stick."

Dalmatic

A liturgical vestment based on a garment from the region of Dalmatia in Eastern Europe. While the chasuble traditionally has one stripe down the middle, the dalmatic typically has two stripes. The Deacon, who is ordained into the Priestly ministry of Christ the servant, wears the dalmatic during formal celebrations.

---

1. *General Instruction*, no. 119.

Humeral Veil

The humeral veil is worn like a shawl over the Priest's shoulders. In the folds of the humeral veil he holds the Monstrance when giving Benediction. The word, humeral, comes from the Latin word *humerus* which means "the upper arm from the shoulder to the elbow."

Miter The miter is the traditional hat of Bishops. It imitates the head covering of the Old Testament Priests. The word, miter, comes from the Greek word *mitra* which means "turban." Sometimes spelled "mitre".

Soutane See *cassock*.

Stole The stole is the mark of spiritual authority. It also reminds us of the Cross of Christ resting and carried on his shoulders. It is worn by Priests, Deacons, and Bishops. The word stole comes from the Latin word *stola*, which means "garment."

Surplice The surplice is a white garment that is worn over the cassock. The surplice is loose, wide sleeved and reaches no farther than the knees. It is worn by clergy in choir and during processions, as well as by altar servers. The word "surplice," comes from the Latin words, *super* and *pellis*, and it means "above the skin."

Vimpa A veil worn over the shoulders of altar servers who, during liturgical functions, hold the Bishop's miter and crozier. Altar servers use the vimpa to avoid direct contact with the miter and crozier, and so show that they do not have the authority of the Bishop. The word "vimpa" comes from the French word *guimpe* which is a narrow flat fabric used for trimming.

Other Vestments

You will sometimes see the *biretta*, the traditional hat worn by clergy. Currently optional for Priests, Deacons, and Seminarians in the Ordinary Form of the Roman Rite, though it continues to be required for Bishops and Cardinals in choir[1]. Even more rarely, you may see the *maniple*, an embroidered band of fabric that hangs from a Priest's left arm. The word comes from the Latin *manipulus*, meaning "a small bundle". It is nowadays rarely worn[2].

---

1. James-Charles Noonan, *The Church Visible: the Ceremonial Life and Protocol of the Roman Catholic Church* (New York: Lewes, 2012), pp. 299–304.
2. Sacred Congregation of Rites, *Tres abhinc annos*, no. 25; *cf.* "Liturgical Vestments and the Vesting Prayers" No. 5, Vatican. Accessed April 27, 2021. http://www.vatican.va/news_services/liturgy/details/ns_lit_doc_20100216_vestizione_en.html. "The maniple … fell into disuse in the years of the post-conciliar reform, even though it was never abrogated."

VIMPA

HUMERAL
VEIL

DALMATIC

COPE BACK

FRONT

MITRE

BIRETTA

Altar Cloth

The white cloth covering the Altar. Sometimes used generically for *altar linens*.

Altar Linens

Any of the various cloths used at the altar. See *corporal, pall, purificator*.

Aspersory

A bucket for containing Holy Water. Also called *aspersorium*.

Aspergillum

An implement used to sprinkle holy water. Also called *aspergill*.

Baldachin

A processional canopy of rich cloth supported by staves and held over the Blessed Sacrament by four Baldachin Bearers when it is carried in procession.

Boat The incense boat is the vessel that contains the incense that will be put into the thurible. Traditionally, this vessel is in the shape of a boat.

Book of the Gospels

Also known as the *Evangeliarium*. The large book which contains the readings from the Holy Gospels to be proclaimed at Mass.

Ciborium

A chalice-like vessel used to contain the Blessed Sacrament, especially in the tabernacle. The word ciborium comes from the Latin word *cibus*, which means "food," and the Greek *kirorion*, which means "cup."

Communion Paten

Also called a *Communion-plate*. A dish-like vessel, normally with a handle, used during the distribution of Holy Communion. When the communicant responds, "Amen," the communion paten is held under the communicant's chin or hands, depending on whether they receive on the tongue or in the hand. The word paten comes from the Latin word *patina*, which means "platter." Not to be confused with a *paten*.

Corporal

A white linen cloth, usually with a cross in the center, used to protect any particles of the Precious Body and Blood of Jesus from falling to the altar cloth. It is always folded and unfolded as to protect any particles from being lost. Corporal comes from the Latin *corpus*, which means "body" as a reminder of the sheet used to hold the crucified body or Our Lord in the tomb.

Crotalus Also called a "clacker" or "clapper", the crotalus is used instead of bells when the bells are to remain silent from Holy Thursday until the *Gloria* of the Easter Vigil. In some parishes, this use is by custom expanded throughout Passiontide, the last two weeks of Lent. The word crotalus derives from the Latin *crotalum*, meaning "rattle".

Evangeliarium

See *Book of the Gospels*.

Funeral Pall

A cloth that covers a casket or coffin at funerals. See also *Pall*.

Lavabo Dish

> The lavabo dish is a shallow dish used when the Priest's hands are washed as he prepares to offer the Eucharistic sacrifice. This act is an ancient symbol for purifying one's soul. *Lavabo* is Latin for "I will wash."

Lectionary

> The book of readings used for the Liturgy of the Word.
>
> It usually contains all the Biblical readings used for the three-year cycle of Sunday Mass readings and/or the two year cycle of daily Mass readings.

Lucifer Combination candle lighter and snuffer. From the Latin word *lucem*, which means "light".

Missal The book containing the prayers said by the Priest during the Mass and the rubrics for celebrating the Mass. The full name of this book is the *Roman Missal* (Latin: *Missale Romanum*).

Monstrance

> A liturgical vessel used to expose the Blessed Sacrament. The word monstrance comes from the Latin word *monstrare*, which means "to show."

Oil of Catechumens

> Olive oil blessed by the Bishop and used to help strengthen a person about to receive the Sacrament of Baptism.

Oil of the Sick

> Olive oil blessed by the Bishop for use in the Sacrament of Anointing of the Sick.

Pall A square piece of cardboard or plastic which is covered by linen and used to cover the chalice. See also *Funeral Pall*.

Paten A small saucer shaped plate of precious metal that holds the Host. Not to be confused with a communion paten. The word paten comes from the Latin word *patina*, which means "platter." See also *Communion Paten*.

Processional Cross

> A crucifix attached to a staff that is about six foot long, used in processions in and out of Mass.

Processional Torch

> A short candle affixed to a long staff. There are many different styles. Usually four or eight of these are carried in Eucharistic Processions, and up to six during the Eucharistic Prayer and Communion during solemn Masses.

Purificator

> A linen cloth used by the Priest or Deacon to dry the chalice after washing and purifying it. Used purificators must always be placed in the proper container for sacred cloths to be laundered.

Pyx   A container used for taking the Blessed Sacrament to those who are sick or homebound. The word pyx comes from the Latin word *pyxis*, which means "box."

Sacred Chrism

> Olive oil mixed with a small amount of balsam, a sweet perfume. The oil is consecrated by a Bishop for use in the sacraments of Baptism, Confirmation, and Holy Orders.

Server Candles

> Candlesticks carried by altar servers in processions, especially during Mass. Each pair of altar servers should have a matching pair of server candles.

Stock   The containers used to hold the *Oil of the Catechumens*, the *Oil of the Sick*, and the *Sacred Chrism*.

Thurible   The thurible is a metal censer that is suspended from one or more chains. Incense is burned in the thurible during liturgies. The word thurible comes from the Latin word *thus*, which means "incense."

Vesperal   Book containing the psalms and prayers for Vespers.

THE CHALICE ASSEMBLY

Chalice A cup of precious metal that holds the wine which becomes the Precious Blood of Jesus after the consecration (figure 1). All chalices should be placed in their proper places after Mass. If the chalices were left unpurified by the Priest or Deacon for some reason, they should be left out for purification by the Priest or Deacon. Never put away an unpurified chalice.

Purificator

The purificator is a sacred linen which is draped over the chalice (figure 2). The purificator is used to clean and dry the chalice. The paten and the communion bread that is to be consecrated sit on top of the purificator (figure 3).

Pall and Corporal

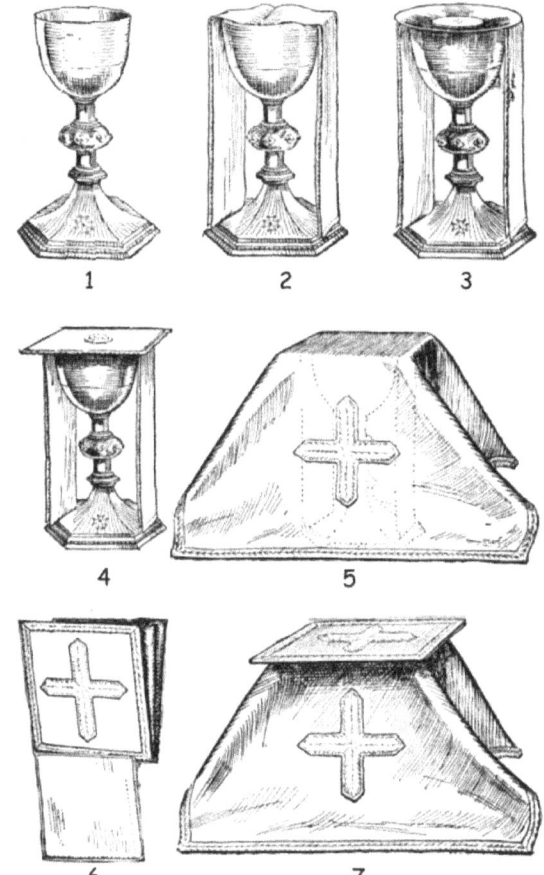

The pall is a stiff square, covered with cloth, used to cover the chalice (figure 4). The chalice is covered to prevent any foreign objects or insects from desecrating the sacred elements.

The corporal is a sacred linen on which the body and blood of Christ are placed. The word corporal comes from the Latin word *corpus*, which means "body."

Chalice Veil and Burse

The chalice veil is a sacred cloth which is used to cover the chalice. The veil is placed over the pall (figure 5).

When vesting the chalice with a veil, a clean corporal is inserted into the burse (figure 6) and placed on top of the chalice veil (figure 7). The burse allows the corporal to lay neatly on the veil.

If the chalice is not vested with the veil, then the corporal is placed directly on top of the pall.

APPENDICES

Appendix 1: Serving at Other Celebrations and Rituals

[Liturgy] condenses into prayer the entire body of religious truth. Indeed, it is nothing else but truth expressed in terms of prayer.

— *Servant of God Romano Guardini (1885–1968)*

Baptisms

By Baptism all sins are forgiven, original sin and all personal sins, as well as all punishment for sin.

(Catechism of the Catholic Church, no. 1263)

Note: Remember to light the Paschal Candle before any Baptismal liturgy.

The sacrament of Baptism can take place during Mass, but it can also be celebrated as a separate ceremony. Either way, the ceremony customarily begins with the procession of the servers and Celebrant from the sacristy to the entrance of the Church, where the Priest welcomes the godparents, family, and child. This first rite includes the naming of the child and claiming him for Christ. The Book Bearer attends the Celebrant[1].

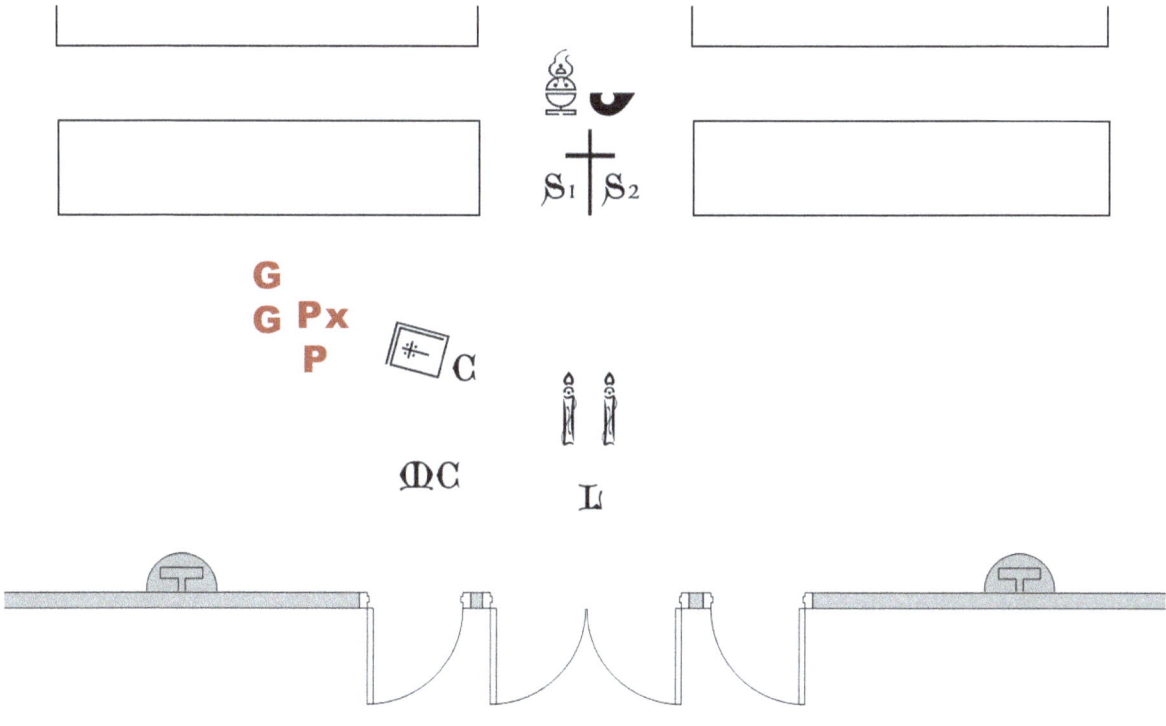

G= Godparent; P=Parent; x=Person to be Baptized

---

1. As in previous diagrams, these represent the layout of a typical church. Your logistics may be different, particularly if the Baptismal font is located at or near the entrance of the church.

When this is done, all take their place in the procession, and Mass begins normally with the Entrance Procession.

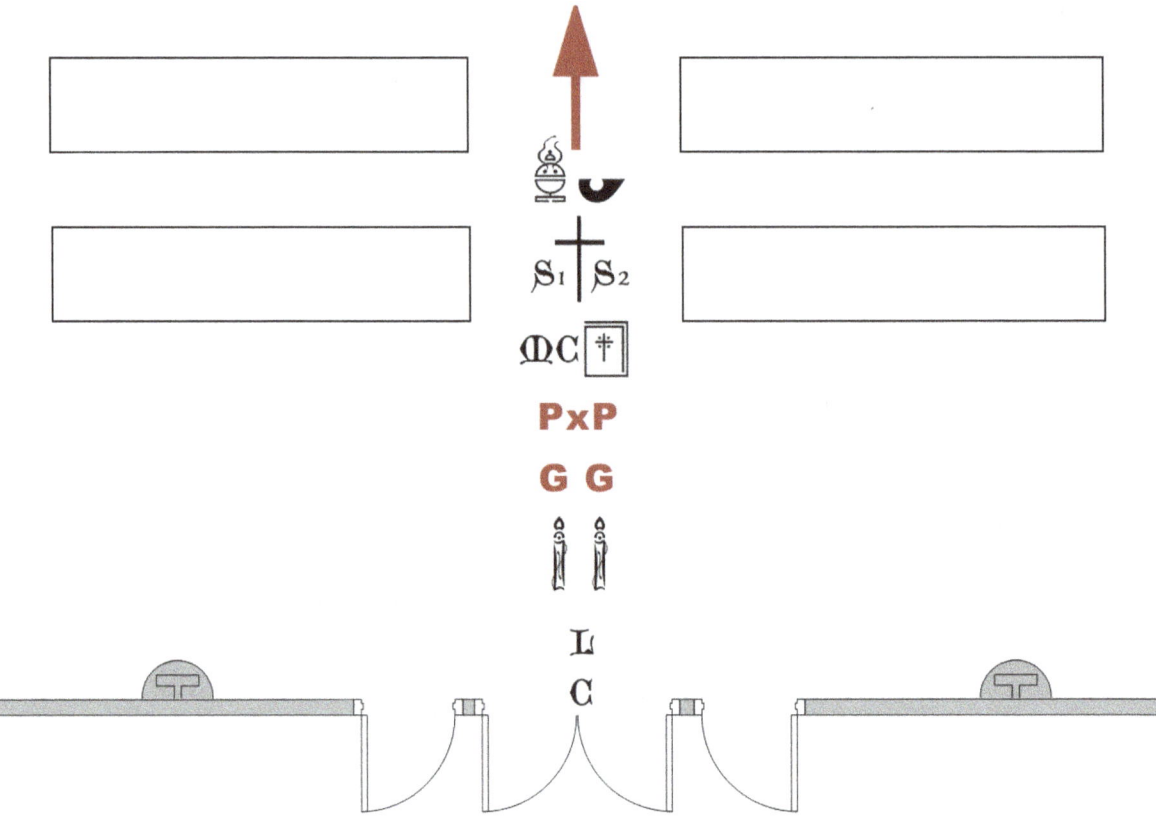

If no Mass is to be celebrated, a short Liturgy of the Word takes place, followed optionally by a homily.

Following the homily, the actual Baptism takes place. The Celebrant (Priest or Deacon), the Book Bearer with the ritual book, and the M.C.[1] process to the Baptismal Font. The Celebrant invites the parents, godparents, and one to be baptized to the font. The Book Bearer holds the ritual book for the Celebrant, while the M.C. hands the Celebrant the various oils, towels, etc. as he needs or requests them.

The rites follow this outline:
- intercessions (Prayer of the Faithful),
- invocation of the saints,
- prayer of exorcism,
- anointing before Baptism with the Oil of Catechumens,
- blessing of the water in the font (except during the Easter season),
- renunciation of sin and Profession of Faith,
- the sacrament of Baptism,

---

1. Or Server 1 where there is no M.C.

- anointing with the Sacred Chrism,
- clothing with the white garment,
- lighting and giving of the baptism candle,
- Ephpheta rite,
- procession to the altar, including the blessing of the mother and father.

WEDDINGS

According to Latin tradition, the spouses as ministers of Christ's grace mutually confer upon each other the sacrament of Matrimony by expressing their consent before the Church.

(Catechism of the Catholic Church, no. 1623)

There are two forms for the celebration of matrimony, the *Nuptial Mass*, where the rite of matrimony is celebrated during Mass, and *Marriage Without Mass*, celebrated with the Liturgy of the Word. In either case, the Matrimony Rite is celebrated after the homily and the Nuptial Blessing is given following the Lord's Prayer.

Order of Celebrating the Nuptial Mass

Introductory Rites
- Entrance Procession / Entrance Antiphon (*Introit*)
- Sign of the Cross and Greeting
- Address to the Couple and those Present
- *Gloria in Excelsis* (Glory to God)
- Collect (Opening Prayer)

The Liturgy of the Word
- Proclamation of the First Reading
- Responsorial Psalm
- Proclamation of the Second Reading (on Sundays and Solemnities)
- Acclamation before the Gospel (*Alleluia*, or tract in Lent), and the Gospel procession
- Proclamation of the Gospel
- Homily

The Celebration of Matrimony
Book Bearer with ritual book and Server 1 with aspersory attend Celebrant.
- Address to the Couple
- The Questions before the Consent the Consent
- The Reception of the Consent
- Blessing and Giving of Rings
- *[Blessing and Giving of the Arras–optional]*
- Hymn or Canticle of Praise

- Profession of Faith (The Nicene Creed; on Sundays and Solemnities)
- Universal Prayer (i.e. the Prayers of the Faithful)

The Liturgy of the Eucharist
- Continue Mass as normal until the Communion Rite.

Communion Rite
- The Lord's Prayer (*Pater Noster* / Our Father)
- *[Blessing and Placing of the Lazo or the Veil—optional]*
- Nuptial Blessing
- Rite of Peace
- Continue Mass as normal.

Concluding Rite
- Solemn Blessing
- Final Blessing
- Dismissal
- Recessional

Order of Celebrating Matrimony without Mass

Introductory Rites
- Entrance Procession / Entrance Antiphon (*Introit*)
- Sign of the Cross and Greeting
- Address to the Couple and those Present
- Collect (Opening Prayer)

The Liturgy of the Word
- Proclamation of the First Reading
- Responsorial Psalm
- Proclamation of the Second Reading (on Sundays and Solemnities)
- Acclamation before the Gospel (*Alleluia*, or tract in Lent), and the Gospel procession
- Proclamation of the Gospel
- Homily

The Celebration of Matrimony
Book Bearer with ritual book and Server 1 with aspersory attend Celebrant.
- Address to the Couple
- The Questions before the Consent the Consent
- The Reception of the Consent
- Blessing and Giving of Rings
- *[Blessing and Giving of the Arras—optional]*
- Hymn or Canticle of Praise

- Universal Prayer (i.e. the Prayers of the Faithful)
- The Lord's Prayer (*Pater Noster* / Our Father)
- *[Blessing and Placing of the Lazo or the Veil–optional]*
- Nuptial Blessing

Concluding Rite
- Final Blessing
- Dismissal
- Recessional

FUNERALS

The Church who, as Mother, has borne the Christian sacramentally in her womb during his earthly pilgrimage, accompanies him at his journey's end, in order to surrender him "into the Father's hands."

(Catechism of the Catholic Church, no. 1683)

NOTE: Remember to light the Paschal Candle before any funeral liturgy.

Altar servers are always expected to serve with dignity and reverence. This particularly important at a funeral Mass, where the friends and family of the deceased can be very emotional and need to feel a sense of peace.

Funeral Masses customarily begin with the procession of the servers and Celebrant from the sacristy to the entrance of the Church, where they meet the casket, pallbearers, and mourners.

As they arrive, the servers back-sweep into the positions shown in the diagram below, so that they can sweep forward following the *Reception of the Body* and process in normal order.

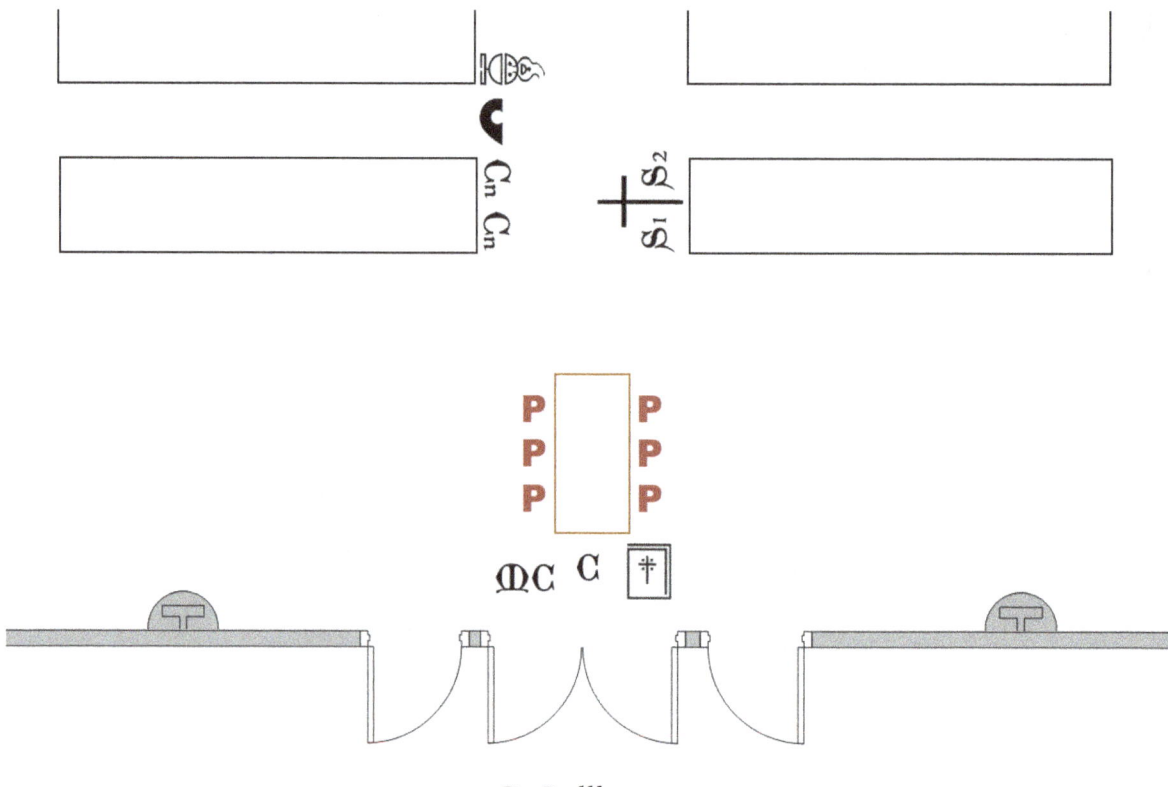

P=Pallbearer

If there is not a server specifically designated to carry the aspersory, the M.C. will do so. In either case, this person and the Book Bearer with the ritual book will attend the Celebrant.

Reception of the Body

The *Introductory Rites* consist of:

- Greeting
- Sprinkling with Holy Water
- *[Placing of the Funeral Pall–optional]*
- Entrance Procession / Entrance Antiphon (*Introit*); the Celebrant(s) are followed by the casket, followed by the mourners.

The Mass

As the servers take their normal places for Mass, a member of the family or the Celebrant may place a Cross or other symbol on the casket. Mass proceeds normally, with specific prayers and readings, until the Prayer after Communion. There follows the *Final Commendation*.

Final Commendation

The funeral director will typically move the casket into position. The Cross Bearer with the Processional Cross, and Server 1 and Server 2 with their candles, take their position at the head of the casket, but about two pews away to give the Celebrant room to walk around the casket. The Celebrant approaches the casket, attended by the Thurifer, the Book Bearer, and the server (or M.C.) with the aspersory.

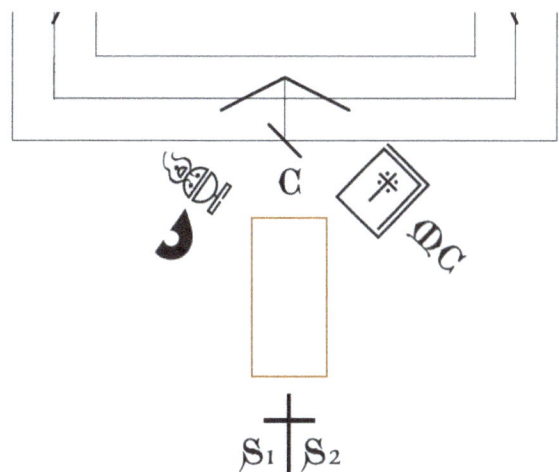

- Invitation to Prayer, followed by silence
- Signs of Farewell: the Celebrant may sprinkle holy water and/or incense the casket. *The Song of Farewell* is ordinarily sung at the same time.
- Song of Farewell
- Prayer of Commendation
- Procession to the Place of Committal; when the Celebrant is finished, he or the M.C. will give the signal to proceed. The procession goes straight out the church doors and to the hearse.

EXPOSITION OF THE BLESSED SACRAMENT AND SOLEMN BENEDICTION

The Eucharist is the supreme proof of the love of Jesus. After this, there is nothing more but Heaven itself.

— Saint Peter Julian Eymard (1811–1868)

Preparation

The Sacristan or M.C. sets out the humeral veil and book or sheet with prayers. Thurible and boat are prepared. Monstrance with flanking candelabras are set out and candelabras lit. The altar is otherwise clear.

NOTE: For both Exposition and Benediction, two or even four Torchbearers may be added. They precede the Celebrant in procession (in pairs), and they flank the Celebrant and other servers at the foot. A Boat Bearer may be paired with the Thurifer if desired.

Exposition of the Blessed Sacrament

A server with the bell and the Thurifer with the thurible and boat precede the Celebrant from the Priest's Vesting Sacristy. When they have cleared the stairs, the bell is rung to signal the people to stand.

When they arrive in position at the foot of the altar, the server with the bell will be on the Priest's left, while the Thurifer will be on his right. The rite follows this outline:

- All genuflect.
- The Celebrant walks into the sanctuary to the tabernacle to obtain the luna holding the Blessed Sacrament. The servers genuflect with the Celebrant.
- The Celebrant installs the luna in the monstrance and genuflects. At this point, the servers kneel.
- The song *O Salutaris Hostia* begins.
- When the Celebrant returns to the foot of the altar, the Thurifer and Boat Bearer (if there is one) stand.
- The Celebrant imposes incense.
- Celebrant and Thurifer (and Boat Bearer) kneel, and the servers hold back the Celebrant's cope.
- The Celebrant incenses the Blessed Sacrament. The servers bow before and after the incensing with the Celebrant.
- The servers release the cope, and the Celebrant hands the thurible back to the Thurifer.
- All stand, then (double) genuflect.
- Servers and Celebrant return to the Vesting Sacristy.

Adoration continues for the appointed time.

Benediction of the Blessed Sacrament

The M.C. (or server) with the bell and the Thurifer with the thurible and boat precede the Celebrant from the sacristy. When they have entered the nave, the bell is rung to signal the people to stand.

When they arrive in position at the foot of the altar, the M.C. (or server) with the bell will be on the Priest's left, while the Thurifer will be on his right. The rite follows this outline:

- All double genuflect.
- The Celebrant, the Thurifer (and Boat Bearer if there is one) remain standing; all other servers kneel.
- The song *Tantum Ergo* begins.
- The Celebrant imposes incense.
- Celebrant and Thurifer kneel, and the nearest servers hold back the Celebrant's cope.
- The Celebrant incenses the Blessed Sacrament. The servers bow before and after the incensing with the Celebrant.
- The servers release the cope, and the Celebrant hands the thurible back to the Thurifer.
- At the end of the *Tantum Ergo* and the acclamation, the Celebrant will say, "Let us pray." The Priest stands for the prayer while the servers remain kneeling. If needed, the M.C. with the prayer book or sheet will stand to attend the Celebrant.
- At the end of the prayer, the M.C. retrieves the Humeral veil. Servers remain kneeling.
- The M.C. genuflects and then places the Humeral veil over Priest's shoulders.
- The M.C. kneels as the Celebrant goes up onto the altar.
- The Celebrant blesses the congregation. As the Celebrant makes the Sign of the Cross with the monstrance holding the Blessed Sacrament, on three occasions (when the Celebrant has raised the Blessed Sacrament to the top of the "cross", when he has lowered it to the bottom of the "cross", and as he moves it from side to side to make the arm of the "cross"):
  - the Thurifer incenses the Blessed Sacrament, and
  - at the same time, the M.C. rings the bell.
- The Celebrant returns to the foot, and the M.C. stands to meet him for the removal of the Humeral veil.
- The M.C. genuflects and reposes the Humeral veil.
- Celebrant kneels. The M.C. returns to position and kneels.

- Servers remain kneeling for the *Divine Praises.*
- Servers remain kneeling while the Celebrant goes to the Altar to remove the luna from the monstrance and repose it in the tabernacle.
- When the tabernacle is closed, the servers stand.
- The song (customarily *Holy God We Praise Thy Name*) is begun.
- When the Celebrant returns to the foot, all genuflect together and return to the sacristy in the same order as they came.

After Benediction

Particularly when Mass is to follow Benediction, two servers must immediately snuff all candles in the candelabra so that the Sacristan can prepare for Mass.

THE SPRINKLING RITE

Water may be blessed and sprinkled over us before the Liturgy of the Word as a reminder of our Baptism, our sharing in the saving events of the death and Resurrection of the Lord, and as a sign of sorrow for sin and protection from evil.

(Ceremonies Explained for Servers, no. 334)

Preparation

Sacristan or M.C. prepare *Roman Missal* or folder, aspersory, and aspergillum. If the rite is to be celebrated as part of the Mass, the aspersory will contain plain water, and a small dish containing about a tablespoon of salt is required. If the rite is to be celebrated before Mass, the aspersory will contain holy water, and no salt is required.

As Part of Mass

During the Easter Season, many parishes celebrate the Sprinkling Rite as found in the *Roman Missal*[1] at weekend Masses. This is celebrated during the Mass in place of the Penitential Rite.

The Book Bearer with the *Missal*, Server 1 with the aspersory, and Server 2 attend the Priest at the chair. The rite follows this outline:
- Introduction to the blessing and invitation to prayer.
- Blessing of the water.
- Blessing and mingling of salt in the holy water.
- Sprinkling of clergy and servers.
- Priest with servers attending walks through the church and sprinkles the people.
- Concluding prayer at the chair.

---

1. *Roman Missal*, Appendix II, pp. 1453–1456.

Appendix 1: Serving At Other Celebrations And Rituals

Before Mass

There are two possible options for celebrating the Sprinkling Rite before Mass. Both begin in a similar way to Benediction, with a bell and two servers preceding the Priest from the sacristy.

Option A: from the Roman Missal

The first option is as found in the *Roman Missal*, as above. One server carries the folder with the text of the rite, while the other carries the aspersory with water and a small dish with about a tablespoon of salt. Once they have entered and genuflected (or bowed), they enter the sanctuary and proceed to the chair. The rite proceeds exactly as above.

Option B: the Traditional Asperges as a Paraliturgical Rite

Some pastors may prefer the alternative method of celebrating the traditional *asperges* sprinkling rite[1]. One server carries the folder with the text and music of the rite, while the other carries the aspersory with previously blessed holy water.

When they arrive in position at the foot of the altar, the server with the folder will be on the Priest's left, while the server with the aspersory will be on his right. The rite follows this outline:

- All genuflect, then kneel, the servers holding back the Celebrant's cope.
- While the choir begins the singing of the *Asperges me*, the Celebrant:
    - sprinkles the altar (three times),
    - crosses himself with the aspergillum, then
    - sprinkles the servers on his right and left.
- The servers release the cope, then all stand and genuflect.
- Celebrant and servers turn around, and the servers again hold back the cope.
- Celebrant with servers attending walks through the church and sprinkles the people.
- When finished, they return to the foot, genuflect, and remain standing.
- When the choir is finished singing the *Asperges me*, the Celebrant and people pray the response and then the final prayer.
- All genuflect together and return to the sacristy.

---

1. Our parish of Holy Rosary had this custom, dating back to the 1980s during our days as a Benedictine parish. This is properly a "paraliturgical rite". Paraliturgical celebrations are those which draw on the ceremonies and the form of liturgical celebrations but are not strictly speaking liturgies.

The Stations of the Cross

The Way of the Cross is the road which leads to Paradise; it is the stairway to holiness. The Passion of Christ is the greatest and most stupendous work of Divine Love.

– Saint Paul of the Cross (1694–1775)

Many parishes celebrate the Stations of the Cross on the Fridays of Lent and on Good Friday. Three servers are needed for this rite: a Cross Bearer and two Torchbearers.

Preparation

Light the altar candles fifteen minutes before scheduled start of Stations. For most Fridays, this will be two candles, but on Good Friday light six. A few minutes before the start of Stations, light the torches.

The Cross Bearer flanked by the Torchbearers precedes the Celebrant from the sacristy. Proceed as shown in the diagram, so that the Cross Bearer ends in the aisle of the nave and the torchbearers flank the Celebrant at the foot of the altar:

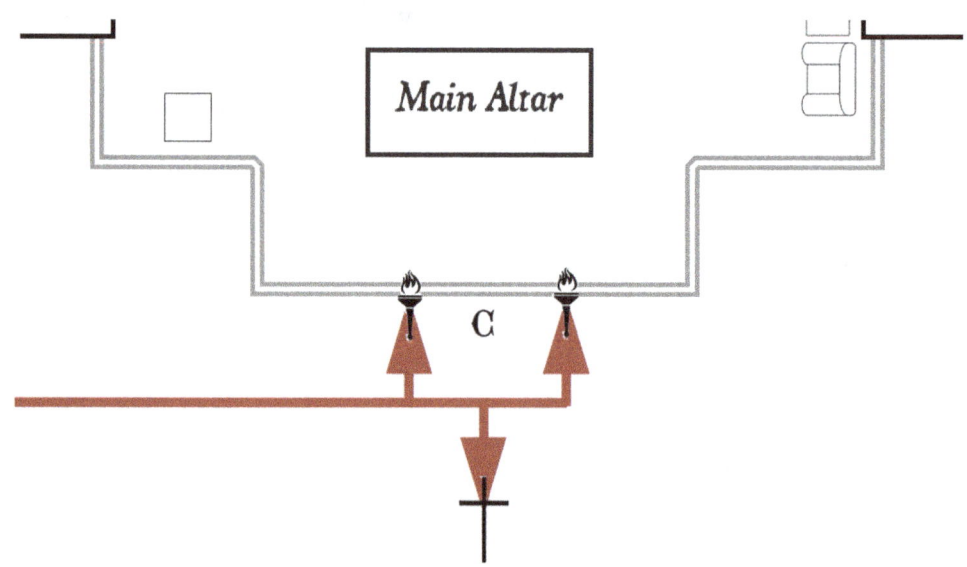

Stations of the Cross: Opening Prayer Position

The rite follows this outline:
- All genuflect, then the Celebrant and Torchbearers kneel.
- Opening prayer.
- All stand. Servers form up and lead Celebrant to the First Station. They face the Station, standing back with plenty of room for the Celebrant to move in front of them.
- The procedure for each station is:
  - The servers stand directly in front of and facing the station, with their back up against the pew.

- Maintain this formation until the readings and prayers are finished and the music begins.
- Then process to the next station and continue doing the same thing at each station and until you reach the 14th station. Be sure to bow when you cross in front of the tabernacle after the 7th station.

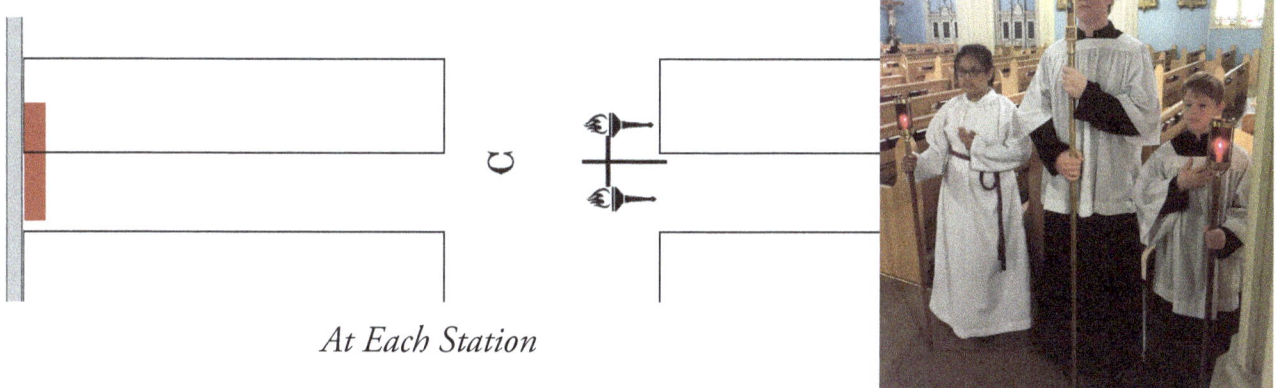

At Each Station

- After the 14th station, go back where to you started at the steps in front of the altar. Torchbearers kneel for the final prayers.
- The Celebrant leads the final prayers. If the Celebrant is a Priest or Deacon, he will impart a blessing.
- All stand. Servers form up and lead Celebrant back to the sacristy.

Appendix 2: Serving Ad Orientem

Despite all the variations in practice that have taken place far into the second millennium, one thing has remained clear for the whole of Christendom: praying toward the east is a tradition that goes back to the beginning.

— Pope Benedict XVI

Introduction to Ad Orientem

Upon occasion, you may be called to assist at a Mass celebrated *ad Orientem* (towards the East) or as most people wrongly say "with the Priest's back to the people".

The point of facing east together is to emphasize the essential character of the liturgy: that of a procession out of time and into eternity in Heaven. We see and taste this procession in the course of the Mass. The Celebrant, standing in the person of Christ, leads the way, but we are all moving together, as a community and as the people of God, as part of the same procession that begins at the Entrance Procession, continues though the Offertory, and culminates with our reception of Holy Communion.

Because you are using the high altar, placement of altar servers for the Mass is different from what you would normally do. The movements are similar, however, and the diagrams below summarize the differences.

Servers and clergy enter the sanctuary as usual, with all going to stand at their seats except the Celebrant, M.C., Thurifer, and Boat, who proceed to the high altar as indicated in preparation of the incensing of the altar.

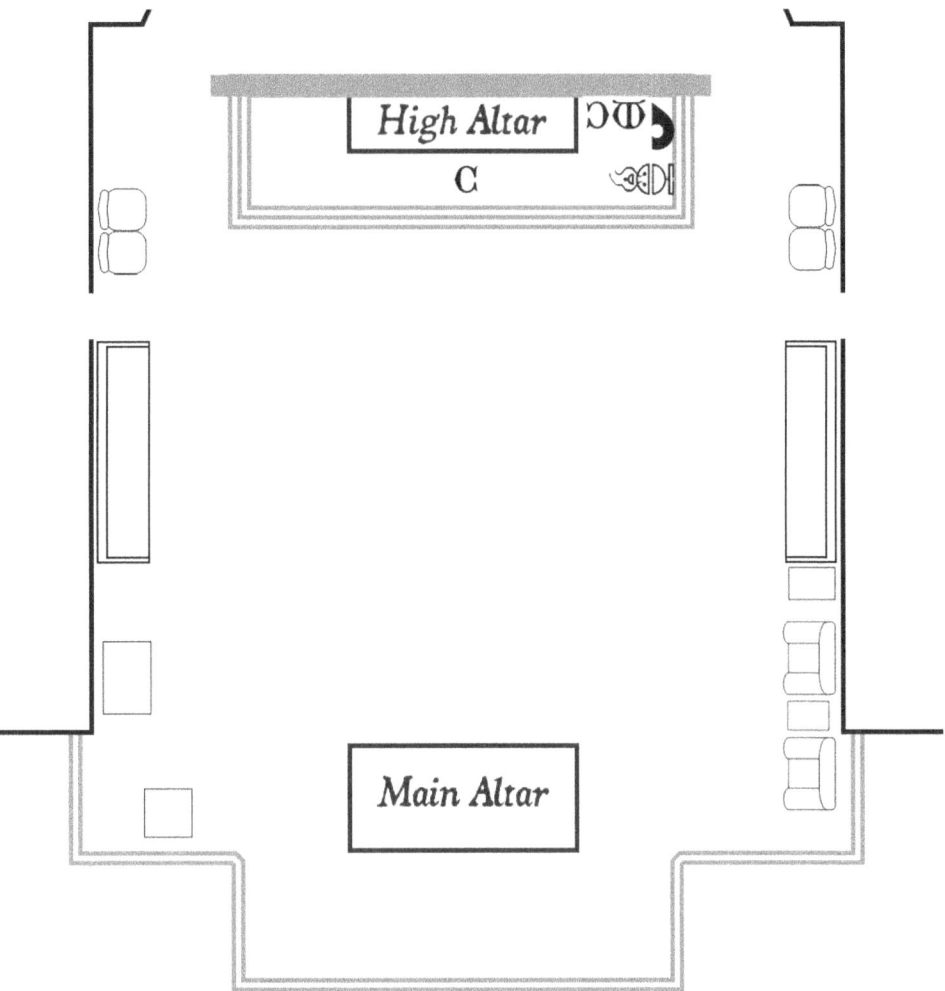

Following the incensing, the Thurifer and Boat bearer retire the thurible and boat as usual, while the Celebrant and M.C. return to their seats for the Introductory Rites.

FOUR CANDLE GOSPEL PROCESSION

From the Sacristy to the Imposition of Incense

The procession splits, with the Thurifer (and Boat Bearer) and M.C. approaching the Deacon and the Priest Celebrant for the imposition of the incense. Meanwhile, Server 1 and 2 with candles, followed by the two Candle Bearers, take up their positions in front of the altar.

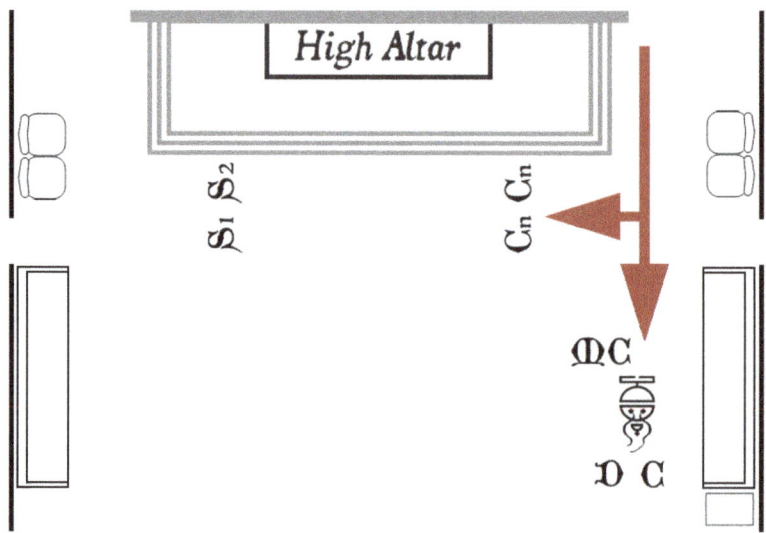

Gospel Procession at the Altar

The Thurifer, followed by the Deacon and then the M.C. solemnly process to their positions at the altar, as shown in the diagram. The Deacon obtains the Book of the Gospels from the altar and shows it to the people.

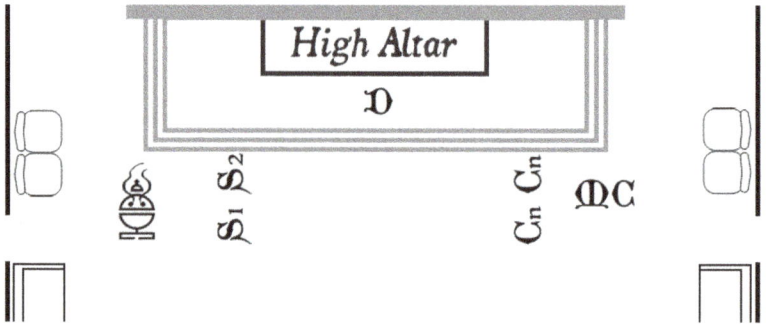

Gospel Procession from the Altar to the Ambo

The Thurifer leads the procession, but near the ambo steps aside to allow the candles and Deacon to pass by.

The Gospel procession makes use of the Box Formation (see "Walking in Formation" on page 21). Server 1 and Server 2 are temporarily paired with a Candle Bearer as they walk toward the ambo, with the Deacon at the center of the "box".

As the M.C. approaches, the Thurifer turns toward the ambo again and pairs up with the M.C. The candles take their position on either side of the ambo as normal.

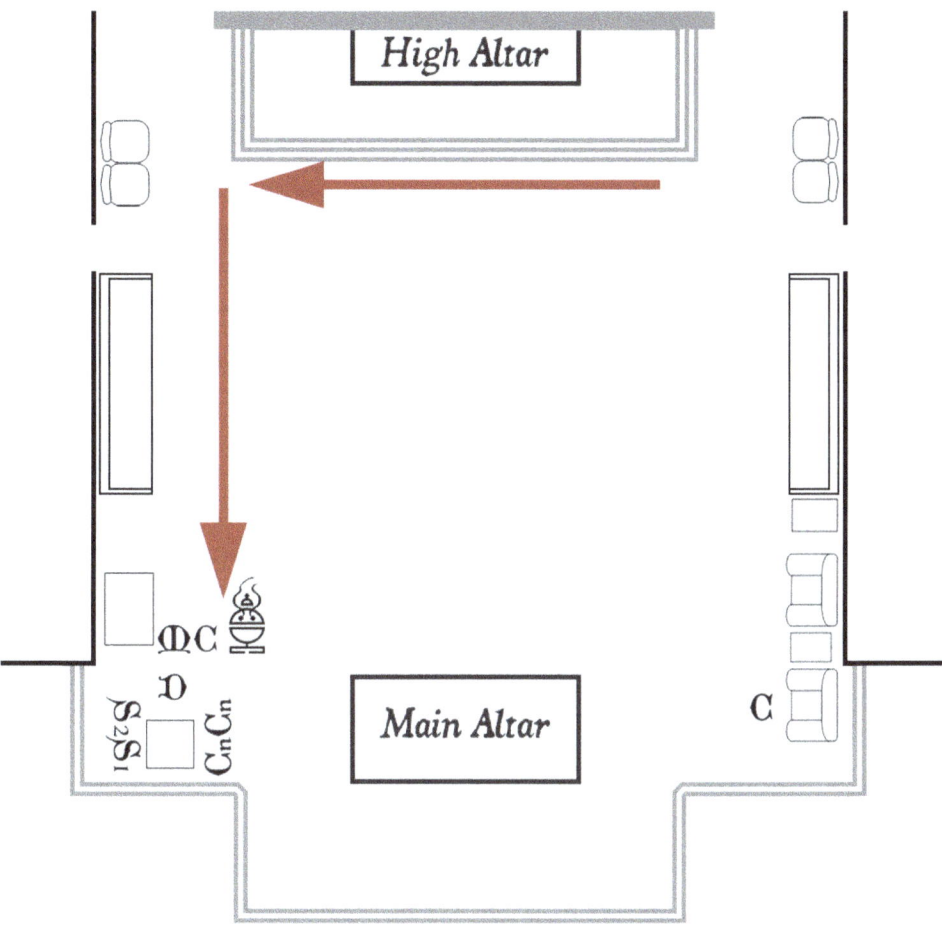

After the Gospel

At the words "the Gospel of the Lord", respond "Praise to you, Lord Jesus Christ." Then, turn towards the sacristy, and return there by the shortest route.

ARRANGING THE ALTAR

Approaching the Altar

Led by the Book Bearer with the Missal stand, Server 1 (with the chalice assembly) and Server 2 (with any additional chalices or patens) proceed in triangle formation.

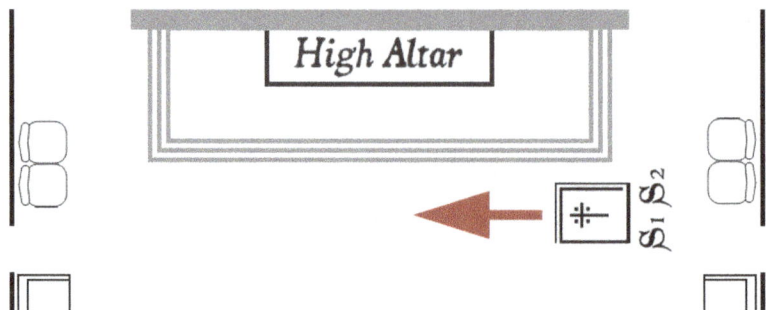

Server 1 and 2 sweep into place, so that all three servers are lined up facing the altar. At a signal from Server 1, all bow and then ascend the steps to the altar. The Book Bearer places the Missal stand while Server 1 and 2 set the altar in the normal way.

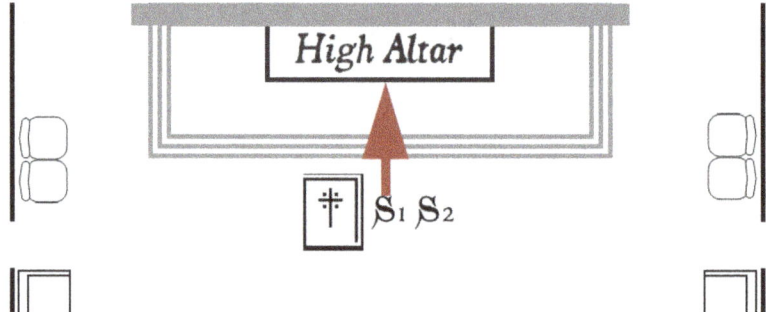

Leaving the Altar

When the altar is set, at a signal from Server 1, all turn and return down the steps. Server 2 should have the chalice veil and burse as normal.

At Server 1's signal, turn back toward the altar and bow.

After the bow, the Book Bearer turns and walks to the seats at the north side of the sanctuary. Server 1 and 2, however, sweep back and return to the credence table.

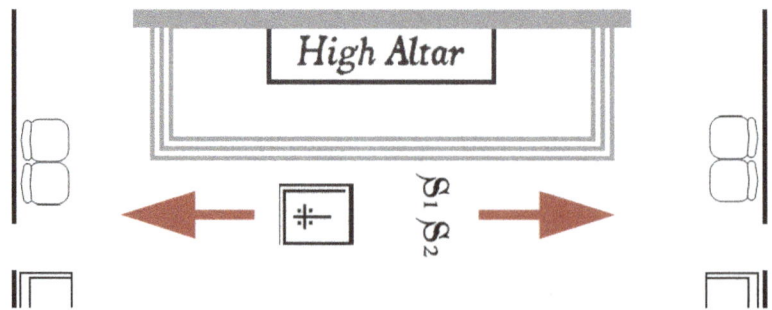

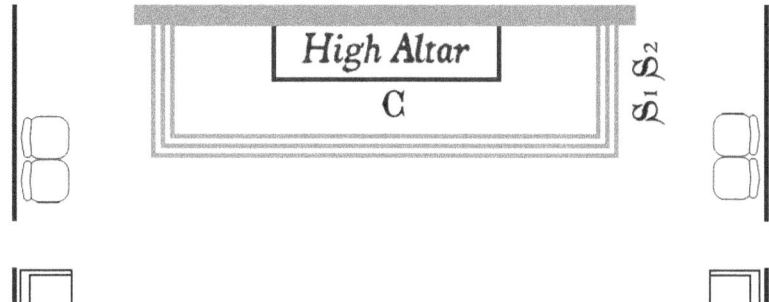

THE EUCHARISTIC PRAYER

During the Eucharistic Prayer, most servers remain standing (and then kneeling) at their seats. The exceptions are noted in the diagram.

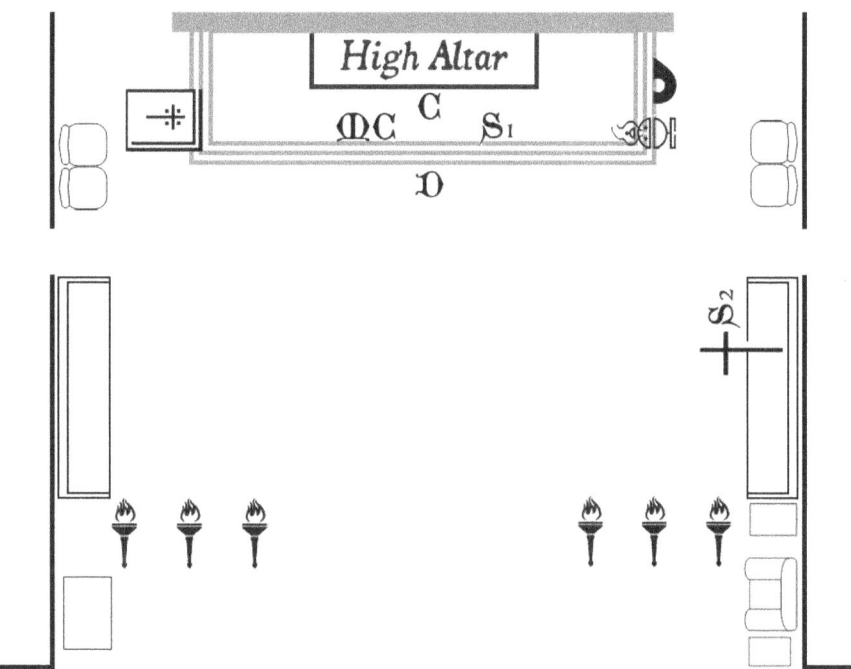

The Book Bearer maintains his position so to be able to remove the Missal during the incensing of the altar and the gifts, and to return it afterwards.

Server 2 must remember to fetch the bells.

As at any Mass, Server 1 moves to the altar and the Thurifer and Torchbearers move into position at the *Sanctus*. All kneel.

Following the Great Amen, all servers stand and Server 1 returns to stand at his seat.

Following the Celebrant's communion, at the bell, all servers go to their Communion positions in the following diagram.

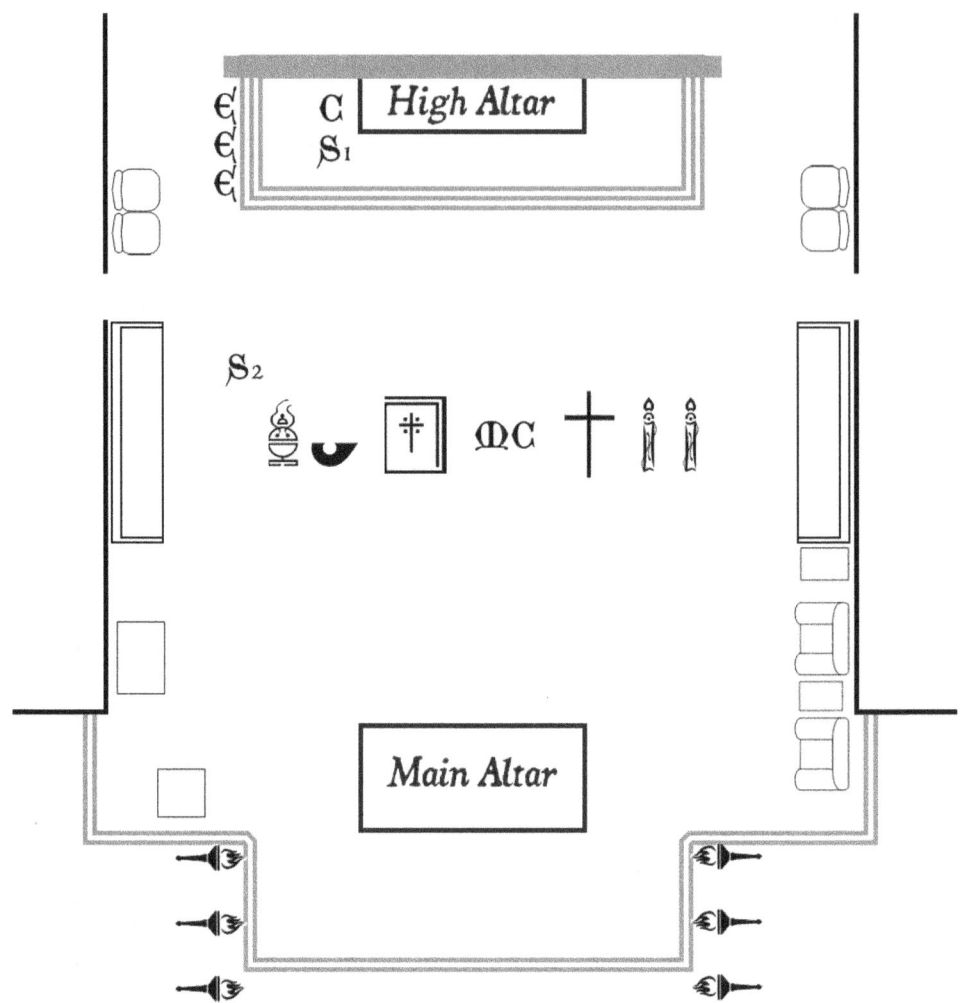

APPENDIX 3: VESPERS

Pastors of souls should see to it that the chief hours, especially Vespers, are celebrated in common in church on Sundays and the more solemn feasts. And the laity, too, are encouraged to recite the divine office, either with the Priests, or among themselves, or even individually.

(Sacrosanctum Concilium 100)

INTRODUCTION TO VESPERS

ALSO KNOWN AS *EVENING PRAYER*, VESPERS is part of *the Liturgy of the Hours*. The Liturgy of the Hours is the pre-eminent prayer of the Church–our main liturgy after the Mass–with specific psalms and prayers at different hours of the day. Like the Mass, Vespers may be said or sung. Normally, Sunday Vespers is to be chanted.

How Do I Pray Vespers?

All you really need to do is follow the rubrics in red and chant along with the words in black. We pray the psalms of the day, alternating stanzas between those seated on the south side of the church (Side 1), and those on the north (Side 2). The Presider, normally a Priest or Deacon, leads us in the prayers.

ALTAR SERVERS REQUIRED FOR VESPERS

In the plainest forms of Vespers, no servers at all are required; it may be prayed individually and in silence. Public Vespers comes in three progressively more solemn variations: *Simple Vespers, Solemn Vespers,* and *Pontifical Vespers.* The form presented here is a type of *Solemn Vespers*, and in addition to the Presider and M.C., it may have the following altar servers:

- Cross Bearer
- Two Candle Bearers
- Thurifer
- Book Bearer

If fewer altar servers are available, the Cross Bearer can double as the Thurifer. If needed, one or both of the Candle Bearers may be omitted.

BEFORE VESPERS

Arrive in the sacristy 30 minutes before Vespers and complete these tasks within the first fifteen minutes:

- Sign in and be vested, having said the vesting prayers.
- Candle Bearers light Altar candles in the usual way.
- Thurifer lights the coals in the thurible.

During Vespers

Genuflect!

Since we are not celebrating the Mass, when crossing in front of the tabernacle, you must *genuflect to the tabernacle*, or bow to it if you are carrying something.

Procession

The Procession is done without a hymn. Organ music or a silent procession are both possible. In any case, the Cross Bearer begins on a signal from the M.C. or Presider.

Procession Variations

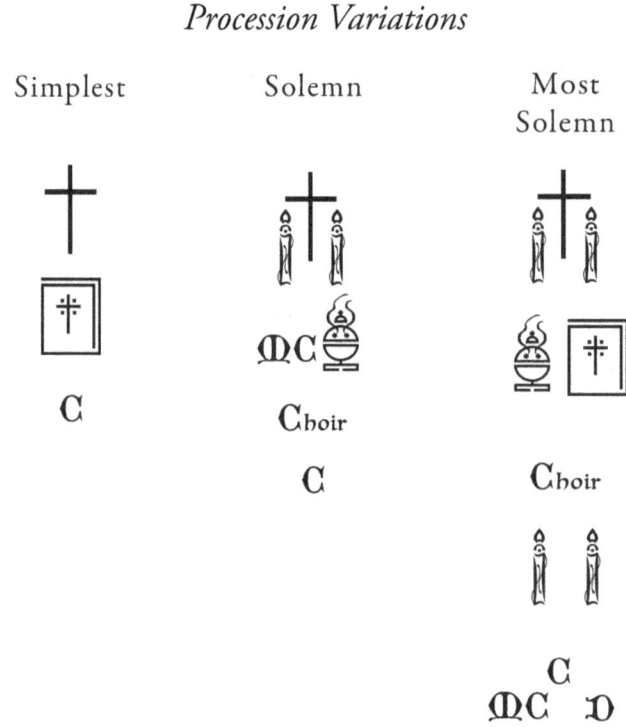

NOTE: the Thurifer does *not* process with the thurible.

All altar servers (and choir members) process in pairs. Each group or pair of servers genuflects or bows as appropriate upon arrival and then enters the sanctuary to repose their items and go to their seats. Remain standing at your seats.

Book Bearer[1]: Bring the *Vesperal* to the Presider as soon as he is in position.

---

1.   If there is no Book Bearer, the M.C. serves.

Opening Versicle and Response

Vespers begins with the opening versicle and response. All altar servers chant the response.

All altar servers make a profound bow to the tabernacle during the words "Glory to the Father and to the Son and to the Holy Spirit" (except the Book Bearer, who bows his head).

Hymn

Book Bearer: hand the *Vesperal* to the Presider and return to your seat.

All altar servers sing the hymn. When the hymn is complete, sit down.

Psalmody

All altar servers join in the chanting of two psalms and one canticle.

All altar servers make a profound bow to the tabernacle during the words "Glory to the Father and to the Son and to the Holy Spirit" each time they occur. This requires standing on the final line of the psalm or canticle, and then sitting again just before repeating the antiphon.

Reading

Pay attention during the reading. Be sure to say (or chant) the responsory following it.

Thurifer: At the start of the reading, go to the sacristy and retrieve the thurible and boat.

Gospel Canticle (Magnificat)

1. Thurifer brings thurible and boat to Presider. All stand.
2. Presider charges thurible. Once this is done, Thurifer stations himself to the right of the altar.
3. Book Bearer goes to Presider and takes *Vesperal*. Presider chants antiphon.
4. At the end of the antiphon, Book Bearer places (open) *Vesperal* on table and returns to seat. At this point, the rest of the congregation and altar servers are chanting the repeat of the antiphon and then on to the *Magnificat.*
5. Presider and M.C. go to meet Thurifer. Thurifer hands thurible to Presider.
6. Thurifer and M.C. take corners of Presider's cope while he incenses the altar during the singing of the *Magnificat.*
7. Presider hands thurible to Thurifer. Thurifer incenses Presider.
8. Presider and M.C. return to their seats while Thurifer incenses the people.
9. Thurifer retires the thurible and then returns to seat.

All altar servers make a profound bow to the tabernacle during the words "Glory to the Father and to the Son and to the Holy Spirit".

Intercessions

Book Bearer: Go to Presider. Hold the book for the Presider for the remainder of Vespers.

Lord's Prayer

Cross Bearer: At the start of the Lord's Prayer, return to the sacristy to retrieve the Processional Cross for the recessional.

Collect

Book Bearer: Following the final prayer, return to your seat.

Recessional

The recessional is handled exactly as at Mass, with the Cross Bearer coming out from the sacristy when the Presider begins to move towards the altar.

In many churches, a Marian antiphon may be sung as part of the recessional.

When the Presider and altar servers reach the entrance of the church, the *Prosit* prayer is not offered. Instead, when all are assembled, one (or more) of the altar servers may ask the Presider (if he is a Priest or Deacon) for the blessing in the usual way, "Jube Domine benedicere".

AFTER VESPERS

Candle Bearers: Extinguish the candles in the usual way.

All altar servers divest and return their vestments to the assigned place.

Appendix 4: Additional Resources

Books

Beyond *The General Instruction of the Roman Missal*, if you are more interested in learning about the sacred liturgy, you may wish to consider these books. For even more detailed information, you may wish to seek out the works consulted in the production of this book, listed on the following page. Although we encourage you to get these titles from your local bookstore, all of them are available on Amazon.com.

We cannot recommend Bishop Elliott's books highly enough. They are designed for those planning the sacred liturgy and provide a solid grounding in the practical aspects of celebration. Most suitable for adults.

- Elliott, Most Rev. Peter J. *Ceremonies Explained for Servers: According to the Roman Rite; a Manual for Altar Servers, Acolytes, Sacristans, and Masters of Ceremonies.* San Francisco, CA: Ignatius Press, 2019.

- Elliott, Most Rev. Peter J. *Ceremonies of the Modern Roman Rite: the Eucharist and the Liturgy of the Hours: a Manual for Clergy and All Involved in Liturgical Ministries.* San Francisco, CA: Ignatius Press, 2005.

- Elliott, Most Rev. Peter J. *Ceremonies of the Liturgical Year: According to the Modern Roman Rite; a Manual for Clergy and All Involved in Liturgical Ministries.* San Francisco, CA: Ignatius Press, 2002.

Signs and Symbols

Guardini's little 58-page book talks about the symbols used in the Mass, everything from the Sign of the Cross to kneeling and standing to incense to bells to the altar itself. It's a perfect meditation for servers and those training them on the physical signs of the sacred liturgy. Zachman's book covers the practical and sacred significance of the parts of the church building, as well as the various vestments and objects used within. Highly recommended.

- Guardini, Rev. Romano. *Sacred Signs.* St. Louis, MO: Pio Decimo Press, 1956. Republished on CreateSpace Independent Publishing Platform, 2015.

- Zachman, Andrea. *The Sacred That Surrounds Us: How Everything in a Catholic Church Points to Heaven.* West Chester, PA: Ascension, 2019.

The Liturgy of the Hours

This wonderful little book serves as an excellent introduction to praying the Liturgy of the Hours. The instructions it provides are clear and easy to follow. Suitable for adults and older servers.

- Murray, Seth H. *Lord, Open My Lips: the Liturgy of the Hours as Daily Prayer.* El Sobrante, CA: North bay Books, 2004.

Putting it all Together

Pope Benedict XVI's book on the sacred liturgy remains one of the great introductions to the theology and practice of the sacred liturgy for adults.

- Ratzinger, Joseph Cardinal. *The Spirit of the Liturgy.* San Francisco, CA: Ignatius Press, 2000.

Signs for the Sacristy

Copies of the various sacristy and vesting prayers may be found at *http://zelanti.org/resources/*. PDFs are available for free download, and there is an option to purchase the printed signs and posters.

Sources Consulted

While the following works were consulted in the preparation of this book, any errors are, of course, the author's own.

Benedict XVI, Pope. *Sacramentum Caritatis: Post Synodal Exhortation on the Eucharist.* Boston: Pauline Books & Media, 2007. (Short title) *Sacramentum Caritatis.*

Britt, Dom Matthew, O.S.B. *How to Serve in Simple, Solemn, and Pontifical Functions.* 3rd ed. Charlotte, NC: Tan Books and Publishers, 2008. (Short title) *How to Serve.*

Carmody, Rev. Charles J. *Learning to Serve: a Book for New Altar Boys.* Milwaukee, WI: Bruce, 1961. (Short title) *Learning to Serve.*

Congregation for Divine Worship and the Discipline of the Sacraments. *Compendium on the Eucharist.* Washington, D.C.: United States Conference of Catholic Bishops, 2016.

Congregation for Divine Worship and the Discipline of the Sacraments. *Redemptionis Sacramentum; Instruction on Certain Matters to Be Observed or to Be Avoided Regarding the Most Holy Eucharist.* Boston: Pauline Books & Media, 2004. (Short title) *Redemptionis Sacramentum.*

Elliott, Most Rev. Peter J. *Ceremonies Explained for Servers: According to the Roman Rite; a Manual for Altar Servers, Acolytes, Sacristans, and Masters of Ceremonies.* San Francisco, CA: Ignatius Press, 2019. (Short title) *Ceremonies Explained for Servers.*

Elliott, Most Rev. Peter J. *Ceremonies of the Liturgical Year: According to the Modern Roman Rite; a Manual for Clergy and All Involved in Liturgical Ministries.* San Francisco, CA: Ignatius Press, 2002. (Short title) *Ceremonies of the Liturgical Year.*

Elliott, Most Rev. Peter J. *Ceremonies of the Modern Roman Rite: the Eucharist and the Liturgy of the Hours: a Manual for Clergy and All Involved in Liturgical Ministries.* San Francisco, CA: Ignatius Press, 2005. (Short title) *Ceremonies of the Modern Roman Rite.*

Fortescue, Rev. Adrian, Rev. J.B. O'Connell, and Dom Alcuin Reid, O.S.B. *The Ceremonies of the Roman Rite Described.* 15th ed. London: Burns & Oates, 2009.

International Commission on English in the Liturgy. *Ceremonial of Bishops.* Collegeville, MN: Liturgical Press, 1989.

International Commission on English in the Liturgy. *Documents on the liturgy: 1963–1979: Conciliar, Papal, and Curial Texts.* Collegeville, MN: Liturgical Press, 1982.

International Commission on English in the Liturgy. *The General Instruction of the Roman Missal: including Norms for the distribution and reception of Holy Communion under both kinds in the dioceses of the United States of America and Universal norms on the liturgical year and the general Roman calendar.* Washington, D.C.: United States Conference of Catholic Bishops, 2011. (Short title) *General Instruction.*

International Commission on English in the Liturgy. *The Roman Missal*. 3rd typical ed. Washington D.C.: United States Conference of Catholic Bishops, 2011.

O'Connell, Very Rev. Lawrence. *The Book of Ceremonies*. Milwaukee, WI: Bruce, 1956.

Trimeloni, Rev. Ludovico, and Pietro Siffi. *Compendio di Liturgia Pratica*. Milan: Marietti, 2007.

United States Catholic Conference, *Catechism of the Catholic Church: Revised in Accordance with the Official Latin Text Promulgated by Pope John Paul II*. Washington, DC: Libreria Editrice Vaticana, 2000. (Short title) *Catechism of the Catholic Church*.

United States Conference of Catholic Bishops. "Guidelines for Altar Servers." 2011. Accessed May 21, 2021. http://www.usccb.org/prayer-and-worship/the-mass/frequently-asked-questions/guidelines-for-altar-servers.cfm.

FOR TRAINERS

An Introduction for Altar Server Trainers

The Church's liturgy may, therefore, be considered as a sacred poem, in the framing of which both heaven and earth have taken part, and by which our humanity, redeemed by the blood of the Lamb without spot, rises on the wings of the Spirit even unto the throne of God Himself.

— *Blessed Ildefonso Schuster (1880–1954)*

SERVING AT THE ALTAR IS ONE of the greatest privileges we have as human beings. Doing so in a way that is fitting and reverent can be a challenge. Mistakes will be made. There is nothing perfect this side of heaven. This does not mean, however, that we shouldn't strive for that perfection. Striving for perfection is exactly what we are called to do, not only at the altar but also in the daily reality of trying to live the moral life. The Lord Himself tells us at the end of His Sermon on the Mount "be perfect, as your heavenly Father is perfect"[1]. Strive for perfection, but don't beat yourself up over falling short. Pick yourself up, learn from your mistakes, and carry on. As a trainer of altar servers, you will not be immune from mistakes. I've made plenty, and I hope that I've learned from them. It's my hope that you can learn from my mistakes, too. Before every liturgy and before every training session, I silently pray the same prayer: "Lord, please don't let me screw this up". This is a good place to start.

Be Prayerful

Always start with prayer. In the prologue to his *Holy Rule*, Saint Benedict says "every time you begin a good work, you must pray to Him most earnestly to bring it to perfection"[2]. Start every day, every training session, and every liturgy with personal prayer, and then pray with your altar servers. Pray that the Holy Spirit will guide you in your actions and in your service to the Lord and to His people.

It's also important that various moments of prayer that occur during the course of serving at the altar not be neglected. Stress to your servers the importance of the vesting prayers. Make sure the Priest prays with the servers before Mass. Pray to begin and end every training session.

Be Consultative

Talk to your pastor. Frequently. Make sure he is onboard with any changes you might want to make. If there is a functional liturgy commission in your parish, make sure you are at every meeting. Never surprise your pastor during Mass, and try not to let yourself be surprised by what the other ministry leaders are doing. In particular, you should coordinate and collaborate closely with the choir director. The time to discuss and plan is well before the beginning of any liturgical rite, ideally weeks before.

Be an Altar Server

The best way to learn the ropes of being an altar server is to serve at the altar, and the best way to learn how to train altar servers is to *be* an altar server. Showing is always more effective than telling. When we started our program, the first thing I did was start serving on Sundays. I continued this for nine months before we started our new training program. It was the single best decision I ever made.

---

1. Matthew 5:48 (RSVCE).
2. Saint Benedict, *The Rule of Saint Benedict in English* (Collegeville, MN: Liturgical Press, 1982).

SERVER TRAINING LEVELS

The modern habit of doing ceremonial things unceremoniously is no proof of humility; rather it proves the offender's inability to forget himself in the rite, and his readiness to spoil for every one else the proper pleasure of ritual.

— *C.S. Lewis*

IN THE ALTAR SERVER PROGRAM WE developed at our parish, we established four Training Levels: (0) Apprentice Server, (1) Junior Server, (2) Senior Server, and (3) Master Server. This level indicates the state of advancement that an altar server has attained in their abilities and maturity. We found that this system had a number of positive effects. First, it provides the Priest celebrant and the M.C. with a convenient way to determine which servers might be best for which roles, and which servers might be called upon for leadership positions. Second, it provides structure for the servers. They know who they can go to if they are unsure of something. Likewise, it encourages the more experienced servers to mentor the Apprentices (and Juniors). Finally, it provides servers with visible markers for their maturation in service, a ready-made development plan, and easily identifiable goals to shoot for.

We highly recommend the implementation of this system, or one like it.

APPRENTICE SERVER (LEVEL 0)

Apprentices are those altar servers who have not yet received formal training for Junior Server. In preparation for advancement to Junior Server, the Apprentice shall acquire a working knowledge of the Order of the Mass, as well as basic rubrics, prayers, and responses.

Apprentices usually serve as Additional Server, Candle Bearer, Torchbearer, or Boat Bearer.

JUNIOR SERVER (LEVEL 1)

To be advanced to the Junior Server level, the candidate shall have performed the duties of an Apprentice with excellence in at least 25 liturgies. An assessment shall be administered to determine if the candidate has acquired a working knowledge of the Order of the Mass, as well as its basic rubrics, prayers, and responses. It was our tradition that when an apprentice became a junior server, they would be vested by the M.C. for their first Mass as their new rank.

Junior Servers are trained in the use of the *Missal*, the Processional Cross, and the Communion patens.

Junior Servers usually serve as Book Bearer, Cross Bearer, Candle Bearer, Torchbearer, or Boat Bearer. Particularly advanced Junior Servers may serve as Server 2 or even Server 1.

SENIOR SERVER (LEVEL 2)

To be advanced to the Senior Server level, the candidate shall have performed the duties of Junior Server with excellence in at least 35 liturgies. An assessment shall be administered to determine if the candidate knows how to serve appropriately.

Senior Servers are trained in arranging and clearing the Altar, as well as with the Thurible, and how to serve at Adoration and Benediction.

In addition to the duties of a Junior Server, Senior Servers may serve as Thurifer, Server 1, and Server 2.

Master Server (Level 3)

To be advanced to the Master Server level, the candidate shall have performed the duties of Senior Server with excellence in at least 45 liturgies. An assessment shall be administered to determine if the candidate has mastered serving in all capacities. The Master Server must know all assignments well enough to teach others. Very few servers ever rise to this level. In the seven years this program was in place at our parish, we only ever had five servers become Masters—and one of those went on to be ordained a Deacon.

In addition to the duties of a Senior Server, Master Servers may be asked to assist the Priest or M.C. with special assignments during complicated liturgical rites.

NOTE   A Senior or Master Server who has proven their reliability, intelligence, and reverence while attending the Priest Celebrant at the Altar may be advanced, at the discretion of the pastor, to study and be trained to function as a Master of Ceremonies (M.C.).

Altar Server Vesture

It is often helpful for the celebrating Priest and the M.C. to be able to distinguish more experienced servers at a glance. Therefore, we vested our Apprentices in a different manner from our other servers. Also, since serving at the altar is traditionally one of the ways to help the young to discern a vocation to the Priesthood or the religious life, it is entirely appropriate to have different vesture for boys and for girls.

Our method, detailed more fully in the "Training Level Summary Chart" on page 134, was to vest Apprentice Servers in alb with white cincture, and when they are more experienced to vest males in cassock and surplice and females in alb with a cincture the colour of the liturgical season or day. We had a small number of hooded albs, which we also used to distinguish our female Senior and Master Servers.

NOTE: Although our parish did not own any albs with lace, it would be entirely appropriate for female Master Servers to wear them as a parallel to males wearing laced surplices.

Apprentices
Vest in alb and white cincture.

Ladies (Junior, Senior, Master Servers)
Vest in an alb with a cincture of the colour of the season or day (see "Liturgical Colors" on page 12).
- Master Servers vest in the hooded albs.
- Master Servers wear the Medal of Saint Benedict.

Gentlemen (Junior, Senior, Master Servers)
Vest in choir dress (cassock and surplice).
- Master Servers may vest in lace surplice, unless the Priest is vested in black or violet, or a funeral Mass is being celebrated.
- Master Servers wear the Medal of Saint Benedict.

TRAINING LEVEL SUMMARY CHART

Training Level	Apprentice	Junior Server	Senior Server	Master Server
Knows	Working knowledge of the Order of the Mass, as well as basic rubrics, prayers, and responses	Use of candles, the *Missal*, the Processional Cross, and Communion patens.	Arranging and Clearing the Altar, proper use of bells, thurible, how to serve at Exposition / Benediction	All ordinary duties, and well enough to teach them to others.
Is Learning	Use of Candles, the *Missal*, the Processional Cross, and Communion patens.	Arranging and Clearing the Altar, proper use of bells, thurible, how to serve at Exposition / Benediction	How to serve at Pontifical Masses. Leadership.	M.C. duties.
Scheduled As*	• Additional Server, • Boat Bearer, • Candle Bearer, • Torchbearer	As Apprentice, plus: • Book Bearer, • Cross Bearer, • Server 2, • Torch Lead	As Junior, plus: • Server 1, • Thurifer • M.C.-2	As Senior, plus: • M.C., • Special assignments
Liturgies until Next Assessment	25	35	45	—
Vesting	Albs and white cinctures.	*Ladies:* • Albs and coloured cincture for the liturgical season or day. • Violet cinctures for funerals. • Gold cinctures when the Priest wears white (except funerals). *Gentlemen:* • Cassock and surplice.		As Senior, but adding the Medal of Saint Benedict. At the discretion of the M.C., may wear lace surplice or alb, except when the liturgical colour is violet or black.

* Normally Apprentices would not appear on the schedule until they are close to their assessment.

Servers should receive proper formation before they begin to function. The formation should include instruction on the Mass and its parts and their meaning, the various objects used in the liturgy (their names and use), and the various functions of the server during the Mass and other liturgical celebrations. Servers should also receive appropriate guidance on maintaining proper decorum and attire when serving Mass and other functions. — *United States Conference of Catholic Bishops*

ANYTHING YOU WISH TO DO WELL, you must first practice. And before you can practice, you must learn. Serving at the altar is no different. Without training and drill, altar servers can become less useful to the Priest celebrant, or worse yet, a distraction to him or to the assembly. The training regime proposed here is designed to start with the basics, and then to build upon them gradually over time. Train the apprentices in the common ceremonial actions, and then let them acclimatize to serving at the altar before moving on to the more advanced server skills.

INITIAL TRAINING FOR NEW APPRENTICE SERVERS

While many parishes have decided to restrict altar serving to older children, the Church in her wisdom tells us that to serve at the altar, the requirements are simply that "Servers should be mature enough to understand their responsibilities and to carry them out well and with appropriate reverence. They should have already received holy communion for the first time and normally receive the eucharist whenever they participate in the liturgy."[1]

Most of those who were trained as apprentices at our parish were therefore very young, and we always tried to schedule an information session for parents and an apprentice server training a week or two after First Communions were celebrated. If possible, you should arrange a visit to the First Communion class *before* they receive the Sacrament to talk with them and their parents about serving at the altar. I also found it helpful to consult with the folks responsible for teaching the First Communion class to help get a bead on who was mature enough and who wasn't.

Scheduling the Training

While it wasn't always possible, we tried to hold new altar server training on a quarterly basis. Talk with your pastor about how he would like to approach this. It's a delicate balance between having new server training too frequently and not frequently enough.

Monthly Meetings

In addition to the quarterly trainings, we had monthly meetings for all servers. Meetings normally consisted of pizza coupled any new information that needed to be shared with the servers, followed by optional training sessions. "New information" could be anything from schedule adjustments to changing procedures to previews of upcoming seasonal or festive liturgies. Sometimes we had activities or games, especially if it was summer and we could be outside on the parish grounds.

These meetings are important in building your server community, as well as providing an important point of contact between the altar server volunteers and staff and the server parents. Make them regular events, and make them fun.

---

1. "Guidelines for Altar Servers", no. 3.

The Three Rules for Altar Servers

During initial training, we normally introduce the "Three Rules for Altar Servers". These are meant to be fun, but also to set the tone for the young Apprentices. It's amazing how these rules stick with them; they really do much to instill the baseline of server decorum in neophyte servers. Repeat these rules during every Apprentice training. When a server violates one of the rules, for example rule 2, always ask (but gently) "what is rule 2?" They might be silly, but they stick. And they're important.

Rule Zero: Pray the Mass!

Before getting to rules 1, 2, and 3 we must discuss the overarching rule, the rule that governs everything we do when serving at the altar: *pray the Mass!* If you are not praying the Mass with the celebrant and the people, you've got no business doing anything else in the sanctuary. Yes, altar servers pray the Mass in a particular way, playing particular roles that neither the Priest nor the people do, but ultimately we are all just fulfilling our various parts in the great prayer at the heart of everything we do. Pray the Mass!

Rule One: Avoid collisions.

Don't run into each other! In most cases, servers are moving with a partner. Make sure you know where your partner is at all times. The purpose of this rule is to remind servers to maintain situational awareness. Keep an eye on where everybody is and where they're moving to. That does not mean wheeling your head around like a top. Keep your head still but your eyes moving.

Rule Two: Don't set anything on fire that isn't supposed to be on fire.

This rule should be self-explanatory. Above and beyond being aware of your surroundings, servers must keep a special eye out for open flames and lit charcoal. Somebody somewhere will become distracted, and vestments (and carpets!) are flammable. Be the person who puts out the unexpected fire, not the person who starts it.

Rule Three: I Meant to do that.

You will make mistakes–there is nothing perfect this side of heaven. Every single server will make at least one mistake some time in their service at the altar. Mistakes aren't important; most of the time the people in the pews will not notice them. What you do *after* you make your mistake is *very* important, though. Take a moment–a short moment–to collect yourself, and then calmly go about your job. Do not do anything that will call attention to yourself. If you turn the wrong way during a procession, don't immediately hurry to get back to your spot. Instead, take a couple of more steps, execute a smart turn, and walk to the correct place. Hardly anyone will notice a small mistake, but everyone will notice a panicky fix.

When I explain this last rule, I always include an anecdote about a time when I made a mistake and how I recovered from it. I'm sure they're still telling the tale of the time I accidentally kicked the sanctus bells halfway through the sanctuary. When I have senior servers helping in the training, they will often share anecdotes of themselves as well. It builds cameraderie and helps the more nervous servers to relax a bit.

The Rules in Summary

The object of the "Three Rules for Altar Servers" is not to place an additional burden on the new servers, something else to memorize. The rules are meant to provide some humourous, but helpful, guidance on the attitude and decorum that we expect from servers, even the youngest. We want them to be prayerful, to be focused and not let themselves be distracted, to be safe, and to help lead the people deeper into prayer.

Rules for Altar Servers

Rule Zero: Pray the Mass!

Rule 1: Avoid collisions.

Rule 2: Don't set anything on fire that isn't supposed to be on fire.

Rule 3: I meant to do that!

Outline for Apprentice Altar Servers Initial Training Session

This outline is used for the initial training session. It is given in outline form, and then in detail on the following pages. This outline may be photocopied for personal use. I usually have the outline, along with the new server registration forms, in a clipboard when I conduct the training, just to make sure I don't miss anything.

TOUR
1. Prayer before Mass
2. Parts of Church. / Parts of Sanctuary. / On to ... Sacristy
3. Attendance / dress / vesting
4. What size?
5. Vesting prayers.
6. Vest!

MISSAL–rubrics: they're the red bits and they tell the Priest (and servers) what to do

WHAT IS YOUR JOB?
- Not to look cute.
- Not to make your parents proud.
1. to assist the Priest in the Sacrifice of the Mass,
2. to add dignity and solemnity to the rite,
3. to lead the congregation into prayer. **most important**
   - You are a MODEL for the people.
   - pointing/ prayer hands
   - Eyes on the action.
   - Know the responses.
   - *Latin Responses* in Lent and Advent (if applicable).

POSITIONS (ideally this part is done by Senior/Master Servers)
1. "Standing, Sitting, and Kneeling" on page 19.
2. "Walking" on page 21.
3. "The Sign of the Cross" on page 22.
4. "Genuflecting" on page 23. (Hopefully this is review!)
5. "Bowing" on page 26.
6. "Striking the Chest" on page 29.
4. "How to Carry Objects" on page 30. Specifically, teach them to carry:
   - candles
   - torches
   - the processional Cross

PROCESSIONAL

RECESSIONAL

If Time:
- Quick walk-through of Mass
- Ending prayers

Initial Training Session Details

Before You Start

Arrive early and be vested before your trainees arrive. If you plan to set out the various equipment and vestments that you will show the servers, plan for arriving an hour or so before the training is to begin. You should at least set out examples of the server vestments, processional candles, and the *Roman Missal*. Give yourself time to vest, to pray, and to calm your mind.

Why vest for training? It sets expectations: this is a serious job and there's a uniform. I find that it also gives parents confidence in the seriousness of the training. This is not to say that you can't have fun or use humour in your training, but wearing a cassock or an alb definitely establishes a gravity to the training from the outset–to you as well as to your servers.

Parents and trainees will generally begin arriving perhaps fifteen minutes early. Since good record-keeping is essential in a program of this kind, have the parents fill out a registration form with their child while they wait for you to begin. There's a sample registration form in "Appendix: Forms" on page 157. Invite the parents to stay for the training. Let them know how long the training will be. This apprentice training is usually about two hours, though it may run long if you have a large number of trainees. Your server parents are your best partners in this ministry after your pastor. Allay any fears they may have as you chat.

Once you've received their forms, give them a copy of your server handbook and encourage the new apprentices and parents to peruse them while they wait. This generally has the effect of ramping up excitement, but also impresses on them that there's a lot to learn.

Start five minutes late. Why? It gives the new apprentices plenty of time to look at their manual. On a purely practical note, many parents will arrive with their children right at the moment that training is scheduled to begin, or even a few minutes late. This gives them time to fill out the forms.

Tour

Always start your new apprentices with a tour of your church. Start at the front doors, in the narthex if you have one. I usually introduce myself before asking each server their name in turn. Shake their hand. Treat them with dignity and respect. Most of them are terrified; if you slip into the role of a teacher or a coach this will set them at ease. Do not allow over-familiarity. I always introduce myself as Mr. Ryng, never as Thom. I sometimes joke that you can call me by my first name just as soon as your age is half of mine. Since I was in my forties when I started training, this seems about right.

1. Prayer before Mass

If you have the prayer before Mass posted in the narthex, begin with this. The prayer itself may be found on page 5. You may wish to make a poster of this, or to purchase one (see "Signs for the Sacristy" on page 126). The Priest and servers together praying this psalm and antiphon is a beautiful tradition, dating back to medieval times. I'd recommend actually praying the prayer with the servers at this point, just as you would before Mass. Unless your pastor is helping with the training, you will need to step in to his role for this.

If you do not have a poster, or if your pastor prefers to begin Mass with a different prayer with the servers, talk about this and explain any procedures around this.

2. Parts of Church. / Parts of Sanctuary. / On to ... Sacristy

Moving from the back of the church towards the sanctuary, talk about the various parts of the church, their history, how they're used, and their meaning. A good source for learming about this yourself is Andrea Zachman's wonderful little book *The Sacred That Surrounds Us*[1].

When you arrive in the sanctuary, be sure to point out the various pieces of furniture within it. When you arrive at the tabernacle, it's worthwhile to have a short demonstration and lesson on properly genuflecting, particularly when moving across the sanctuary. Have each apprentice practice in turn. Make sure they stop, genuflect, and stand before they start moving again. No drive-by genuflections!

At the altar, be sure to show the apprentices the altar stone and talk about its meaning. If you know the names of the martrys whose relics are contained within, talk about who they were.

Show them the server seating and explain that every position has their own assigned seat.

If there is a separate Priest's vesting sacristy, you should tour that next, if appropriate. We always tried to do this so we could show and explain the various parts of the Priest's vestments.

End your tour in the servers' sacristy. Show them where the various items are kept. Remind them not to worry if they don't remember everything. They can always ask an older server or a responsible adult later.

3. In the Sacristy: Attendance / dress / vesting

Talk about your attendance rules. It's important to set expectations early, and this is why it's useful to have parents present. Our rules were pretty straightforward (see "Attendance" on page 14). Impress on

---

1. Zachman, *The Sacred That Surrounds Us: How Everything in a Catholic Church Points to Heaven* (West Chester, PA: Ascension, 2019).

the apprentices that even though they are not necessarily on the schedule, they should still serve. Here's the quick version:

1. On days when you are scheduled, arrive at church 30 minutes before Mass and vest immediately.
2. If you are scheduled and you can't make it, you are responsible for finding your replacement.
3. If you are not scheduled and you wish to serve, arrive in the sacristy 30 minutes prior to Mass and ask the M.C. if you can serve and in what capacity. For us, the answer was almost always "yes".
4. Apprentices are usually not on the schedule, but they are encouraged to serve at every Mass they attend.

Next, show the servers what vestments they are expected to wear, and talk about how they are to be cared for and hung up when done. Talk about the dress code. Details may be found in "Appropriate Dress" on page 15.

4. What size?

Sizing for altar server vestments is always a challenge. You will never have vestments perfectly fitted to every one of your servers. Do your best! The guidelines are given in "Vesture" on page 16. The most important thing is trying to get the length correct. I always impress on them that the hem of the vestment should just brush the top of their shoes.

Cinctures: the best way to find out if a cincture will fit is to fold it in half, take one end in each hand, and stretch out your arms. If your arms are straight out on either side of your body and there is no sagging in the cincture, you have the correct fit. If you can't stretch out your arms fully, the cincture is too small. If it sags when your arms are fully stretched, it's too long.

5. Vesting prayers.

Show them where the vesting prayers are posted and do a quick walkthrough: take the vestment in hand, make the Sign of the Cross, silently pray the vesting prayer. At this point I mention that traditionally the next step is to kiss the vestment before putting it on. In our program, this was strictly optional, but I always do it. I have found that while few apprentices do this, as servers advance in the program, they are more likely to.

6. Vest!

And now the apprentices vest! This will always take longer than you think it will, because every server needs to find their proper size. Once they do, tell them to remember their size! You will also need to show each server how to tie their cincture. If any of the servers are wearing inappropriate shoes or have a striped shirt that shows through their alb, point them out as reasons there's a dress code.

Always conduct trainings, practices, and rehearsals with vested servers. I find there are fewer shenanigans this way. They will soon learn to adopt a certain seriousness and reverence when they are vested.

Missal

Now that the servers look the part, it's time to start showing them their job! Open the *Roman Missal* on a countertop or table where all the trainees can gather around. Explain what it is briefly and show them some of the pages. Find one that has both red and black text and ask them what it means. The black text of course is the prayers and other things that the Priest says during the Mass. The red text is called *rubrics*, and they're and they tell the Priest (and the servers) what to do. We follow the rubrics, as well as various instructions and handbooks that explain the rubrics. We don't just make this stuff up as we go along! The Church gives us what to do in the Mass and that's what we do!

What Is your Job?

So as an altar server, what is your job? Ask them. Almost every group will get at least one answer correct (usually number 1, below), but it can be informative to hear all of the misconceptions.

Here are some things that are *not* your job:

- You're not up there in the sanctuary to look cute–in fact if you're doing your job properly, most of the time people won't even notice you as an individual.
- You're not even there to make your parents proud–though that's okay if you do.

The job of the server is three-fold:

1. to assist the Priest in the Sacrifice of the Mass,
2. to add dignity and solemnity to the rite, and
3. to lead the congregation deeper into prayer.

This third item is the most important. There will always be somebody in the congregation who is new, or somebody coming back to Church after a long time away, or somebody who is just distracted in the moment. The altar server is a model for the people, a reminder of how to pray. As such, they should never be monkeying around. They should be quiet, attentive, and reverent at all times. Reiterate the three rules.

Show them how to fold their hands in joined hands position (see page 19).

Emphasize that at all times they must keep their eyes on the action: if someone is reading at the ambo, that's where your attention is. If the Priest is at the altar, that's where your focus is. Tell them that it's part of the server's job to make all the correct responses in Mass, to help lead the people in prayer.

Positions

This is really the meat of the new apprentice training.

In an ideal world, this part should be taught by senior/master servers under your supervision. Here's where you teach the new apprentices to stand, sit, walk, and carry things. They might think they know how to do these things. They don't[1].

Go over the "General Rules" on page 18, and then it's on to:

1. "Standing, Sitting, and Kneeling" on page 19.
2. "Walking" on page 21.
3. "The Sign of the Cross" on page 22.
4. "Genuflecting" on page 23. (Hopefully this is review!)
5. "Bowing" on page 26.
6. "Striking the Chest" on page 29.
4. "How to Carry Objects" on page 30. Specifically, teach them to carry
   - candles
   - torches
   - the processional Cross

In each case, model the position or action first, then one by one (or pair by pair) have each trainee follow. Do each of these several times at least, until everybody is comfortable with doing each of these. Remind them that if they forget anything, it's all laid out for them in their book.

After this, your new apprentices should be able to practice processing in for Mass.

---

1. Unless of course, they have an older sibling who has already been trained and is serving. Sometimes these younger siblings come to the apprentice training practically ready for the junior server assessment. If that's the case, you might be able to enlist their aid in helping you to model the various actions.

Processional

It's best to teach this in phases. First, teach the procession as far as the sanctuary, and then teach them to get to their seats and sit down.

Phase 1: to the Sanctuary

Line up your apprentices for typical Sunday entrance procession (see "1: Various Forms of Entrance Procession" on page 40). Be sure you've got servers holding the processional Cross and candles correctly and in the correct position.

Walk them through the procession to their arrival at the sanctuary (see "Option B: Lining Up at the Foot" on page 41). Emphasize that this is no race! They should walk slowly and stay shoulder-to-shoulder with their partner. As they approach the sanctuary, remind them to sweep as they turn. Once they've all arrived at the sanctuary in their proper position, do it again! Cycle each server through the various positions in the procession until everyone has had a turn processing up as a Candle Bearer. If there aren't too many servers, try to make sure everyone has a turn as Cross Bearer, too.

NOTE: If your parish normally uses Option A on Sundays, obviously teach that procedure instead. For this phase of the training, take them as far as reposing their equipment, and then move on to phase 2.

Phase 2: to the Beginning of Mass

After you've decided that they've got this more or less down, proceed to the next step. The easiest way is to start immediately after the last group has processed and is position at the entrance to the sanctuary. As you did before, slowly walk them through the next steps until they are standing in front of the assigned seats (see "3: Preparing for the Introductory Rites" on page 42 and "4: Seating" on page 44). Reset them in their positions at the entrance to the sanctuary and have them do it on their own.

You'll probably have to do this several times. Then, switch everybody's starting position, and do it again. Once you've done this a couple of times, put it all together.

Phase 3: putting it all together

Have the apprentices line up for the entrance procession and go through the entire procession and entrance into the sanctuary until they're standing in front of their seats. Do this at least a couple of times, depending on how you're doing for time.

Recessional

While it's tempting to say that the recessional is just the processional in reverse, it can often be more confusing, particularly when you are learning. Take it slowly, step by step. Repeat several times until everyone has it down.

If There's Time

At this point, you're probably close to or right at your two hours. If you've got fifteen minutes left, and you've got some older servers to help, doing a quick walk-through of the Mass can be extremely helpful. Start with the entrance procession and go right through until the recessional.

Afterwards, talk about the prayer or blessing of the servers after Mass. If it is the custom at your parish for the Priest to use the traditional blessing, it can be found on page 6. If your parish has a different custom, be sure to explain that to the servers and perhaps model it if appropriate.

In any case, try not to run over time if at all possible. End the training with a prayer of thanksgiving and send the servers to divest themselves. Be sure to remind them to put things away neatly and where they belong.

Blessing the Servers at the Start of their Ministry

The Bishops of the United States say that "The Order for the Blessing of Altar Servers, Sacristans, Musicians, and Ushers (*Book of Blessings*, nos. 1847–1870) may be used before servers first begin to function in this ministry"[1]. I would change "may" to "should". On a quarterly basis (right after training) new Apprentice servers should be blessed as they enter into their ministry. All servers, indeed all ministers serving in the parish, should receive the blessing on an annual basis. This might be done at Pentecost or on the fifth Sunday in Ordinary Time, when the readings are particularly appropriate (especially in year C).

SUPPLEMENTAL TRAINING FOR APPRENTICE SERVERS

You will want to have Apprentice Servers know how to do more than stand, sit, and walk. There are two basic methods for supplemental training, and a mature program will probably have a little bit of both. You can do an on-the-spot training for a specific Apprentice who suddenly finds themself drafted into being Book Bearer for the first time, for example. Alternatively (or additionally), you can hold supplemental training sessions, possibly during your monthly server meetings or on a Sunday after Mass.

In any case, there are several things that Apprentices will need to learn, and there just isn't time for everything during their initial training, where they are likely already overwhelmed. These are in rough order of maturity required.

- **Boat Bearer** (probably best learned as an on-the-spot training)
- **Torch Bearer** (one of the first things you should teach an Apprentice)
- **Gospel Procession** (Since this is the thing that actually makes Apprentices useful as Candle Bearers, the sooner they learn this, the better!)
- **Cross Bearer**
- **Book Bearer**
- **Handling Communion Patens** (avoid doing this as an on-the-spot training)

Many of these skills appear on the assessment for Junior Server, so every Apprentice Server will need to learn them at some point. Everybody progresses at their own pace, so make sure to have this training available regularly.

Training Outline

Each of these training sessions works in roughly the same way.

1. Pray.
2. Familiarize apprentices with the equipment. Show them how to hold it and carry it, and let them each practice for a bit. For the Cross and the Gospel Procession candles, this should be a simple review.
3. Explain the duties of the position or job. A good place to start is the section on "Altar Server Duties" on page 55.
4. Model the position or job, if necessary using as helpers servers who already know the position. For example, demonstrate the Gospel Procession from beginning to end. Depending on your servers, you may wish to do this more than once.
5. Walk the trainees through the same procedures once or twice.
6. Have them practice, practice, practice. Switch off positions as appropriate. Praise them when they're doing it right, and gently correct them when they're not.
7. Finish up with a prayer.

---

1. "Guidelines for Altar Servers", no. 11.

TRAINING FOR JUNIOR SERVERS

Training sessions for Junior Servers are best accomplished in bite-sized chunks. We have found this to be a great use of monthly meetings. Each of the skills that Junior Servers must master is a discrete unit, so it's advantageous to hold a monthly half-hour or hour training on each of these subjects in turn:

1. Arranging and clearing the altar / using the bells
2. Being a Thurifer[1]
3. Serving at Exposition and Benediction of the Blessed Sacrament
4. Serving at Stations of the Cross (may also be appropriate for Apprentice Servers)
5. Serving at Weddings
6. Serving at Funerals
7. Serving with a Bishop (as Miter / Crozier / Book Bearer)

The format for these training sessions should roughly follow the outline given in the section on "Supplemental Training for Apprentice Servers".

TRAINING FOR SENIOR SERVERS

By the time a server has been promoted to Senior Server, they will be proficient in arranging and clearing the altar, the proper use of bells, the thurible, and how to serve at Exposition and Benediction and various other rites. They will have served in all capacities, and they will be comfortable doing so. They have modeled proper decorum and behaviour for the younger servers and supported them. They will hopefully have displayed leadership, including helping to train Apprentices and perhaps Juniors. In short, Senior Servers are the backbone of a highly functioning altar server program.

While it is important to train your Senior Servers to properly serve at Pontifical Masses and to set the *Missal*, the most important skill they will have to learn is leadership. If they have not yet demonstrated leadership, it's up to you to help them be comfortable in doing so. They should also "shadow" the M.C. during Mass at least once, and even serve as a secondary M.C. (M.C.-2) during the more complicated liturgies of, for example, Holy Week. For them to be promoted to Master Server, you must have confidence that in your absence, they will be able to lead the other servers at the Mass or at a training and manage any problems that might come up.

ASSESSMENTS

Assessments should be scheduled quarterly or as needed. All assessments must be given by two adults to a single server at a time. Other servers awaiting their turn should be in another room under adult supervision.

All assessments consist of two parts: (a) demonstrating skills used in physically serving in the Mass and other liturgies, and (b) demonstrating knowledge of the various "tools of the trade". This last part should be conducted in the sacristy, if possible. For each item, name it and ask the server to point it out. Suggested assessment forms follow on the next few pages.

---

1. Please note that although Junior Servers are trained in the delicate art of being a Thurifer, it should be a rare occasion indeed that one serves as such! Normally this is a job for a Senior Server, but in a pinch we've been known to use a particularly mature Junior. In all cases, even after Thurifer training, it's a good idea to have the newly-trained server "shadow" and experienced Thurifer by serving at their Boat Bearer. Once they've done this a few times, switch their positions.

Assessment for Junior Server

For the Junior Server assessment, the items indicated on the form (and some additional ones) should be set out on a counter or table.

Assessment for Senior Server

For the Senior Server assessment, set out some items but not all of them. Inform the server that the items they will be asked to identify will either be on the counter or in their proper place in the sacristy.

Assessment for Master Server

The Master Server assessment is substantially different from the others. It consists of a checklist of tasks, undertaken over the course of weeks or months or longer, followed by an assessment session consisting of the Junior and Senior assessments, plus a few additional tasks and questions. For the "tools of the trade" part, all items should be in the places where they are normally kept in the sacristy.

Rehearsal for Palm Sunday

After the Assessment

A score of 80% should be required to pass, though if any major skill is lacking that should be grounds for not passing. After the assessment, thank the server and say that you will give them the results after speaking with the pastor. After the assessments are done, talk with your pastor about how each server did. Some pastors will want to have a conversation, and some will want some sort of written summary. When you and the pastor agree on individual promotions, inform each server individually. If a server did not pass, tell them what they need to do to improve. The answer is rarely "no", but sometimes it's "not yet". If that's the case, schedule another assessment for that server in two months.

Assessment for Junior Server (Level 1)

Working knowledge of the Order of the Mass, as well as basic rubrics, prayers, and responses

Name: **Recommendation:**

Date:

Demonstrate each of the following. If additional servers are required, you may recruit them from the other servers present.

Skill		Notes
Vesting (prayers)	☐	
Stance	☐	
Sign of Cross	☐	
Sit	☐	
Kneel	☐	
Hold candle	☐	
Procession (sweep)	☐	
Gospel Procession	☐	

Answer the following questions to the best of your ability.

Demonstrate a simple genuflection. When is it used?	☐	
What are the different kinds of bow? Give an example of when each would be used.	☐	
What is the dress code?	☐	

Identify tools of trade:

Paten ☐
Communion Paten ☐
Chalice ☐
Missal ☐
Alb ☐
Purificator ☐
Processional Cross (crucifix) ☐
Cruet ☐
Corporal ☐
Sacristy ☐

Assessment for Senior Server (Level 2)

Use of Candles, the Missal, the Processional Cross, and Communion Patens.

Name: **Recommendation:**

Date:

Skill   **Notes**

Demonstrate each of the following. If additional servers are required, you may recruit them from the other servers present.

Skill		Notes
Vesting (prayers)	☐	

Junior Skills   Choose three items from Junior assessment.

	☐	
	☐	
	☐	
Hold Missal	☐	
Carry Missal to Altar	☐	
Light Altar Candles	☐	
Assemble chalice assembly	☐	
Arrange altar	☐	
Clear altar	☐	
Bells - when?	☐	
Bells - demonstrate	☐	
Prepare thurible and charcoal	☐	

Identify tools of trade:

Purificator	☐
Corporal	☐
Lavabo dish	☐
Cruet	☐
Surplice	☐
Pall	☐
Monstrance	☐
Burse	☐
Humeral veil	☐
Sacrarium	☐
Sacristy	☐

Assessment for Master Server (Level 3)

Name: **Recommendation:**

Date:

Pre-assessment Checklist   **Date / Notes**

Serve 45 lituries as senior server	☐	
Serve as secondary MC (MC-2)	☐	
Help train apprentices (2 sessions)	☐	
Help train apprentices (2 sessions)	☐	
Help train juniors (2 sessions)	☐	
Help train juniors (2 sessions)	☐	
Serve Benediction	☐	
Serve Wedding	☐	
Serve Funeral	☐	

Skill   **Notes**

Run through Junior and Senior skill and item assessments, then this one.

Set Missal for specific day	☐	
Talk about a time when there was some sort of problem or emergency during Mass. What happened? What did you do? What would you do differently?	☐	
You are the seniormost server at a Mass. It's fifteen minutes before the start of Mass time, and only one other server has shown up. What do you do?	☐	
Talk about a time when you demonstrated leadership as a server.	☐	
What skills or attitudes do you think are most important for an altar server?	☐	
How's your prayer life?	☐	

Scheduling Servers

There is no exercise which is more pleasing to God, or more meritorious, or which has greater influence in infusing solid piety into the soul, than the assisting at the holy sacrifice of the Mass.

— *Servant of God Dom Prosper Guéranger, OSB (1805–1875)*

THERE ARE MANY WAYS TO SCHEDULE altar servers, and no one way is correct for every parish. A lot is going to depend on how many servers your parish has. We started off with a tiny number: there were weekends where there were simply no servers available at all. As we built up the program, we eventually rose to nearly fifty servers. The most important thing is to communicate the schedule in a clear and consistent way with the parents and the servers.

SUGGESTIONS

Be methodical and plan well in advance. Divide the servers into teams. This way, they will learn to serve with each other. Have a "standard" schedule for your teams, a predictable rotation that stays pretty much the same. Parents will thank you. Send the schedule to the parents at least two weeks before the time period it covers is about to begin. There will always need to be adjustments once the parents actually have the schedule in their hands. Be patient.

HOW WE DID IT

We only had two weekend Masses in our parish, so we were able to divide the servers into three teams: a Vigil Team (V), and alternating A and B teams for Sundays. We were also paired with another parish, also under our pastor, so we could occasionally borrow servers (and loan them out!) when there were shortages caused by vacation or illness. We also had a small number of "floaters": servers who weren't on any team but functioned as a sort of ready reserve.

In some situations, usually big feasts or during the summer vacation times, we would simply ask for volunteers to fill the gaps in the schedule before we finalized it.

We tried to have the schedules cover liturgical seasons, or reasonably large fractions thereof:
- Advent and Christmas
- Winter
- Lent and Holy Week
- Easter Season
- Summer
- Autumn

A sample schedule is reproduced on the following pages. I deliberately chose the most complicated time of the year. As you study the example, you will notice some of the challenges our parish had to deal with. Wherever you see a blue box, this indicates an empty slot that we were unable to fill by the time the schedule was sent to parents. On some days positions were doubled up, most often the Book Bearer would also serve as Crucifer. Often on the actual day, those spots would be filled by one of our floaters or by unscheduled Apprentices.

SERVERS SUGGESTED FOR VARIOUS CELEBRATIONS

The suggested servers for many liturgical celebrations may be found in "Progressive Solemnity" on page 11. The information below expands on this.

The Mass

Major Solemnities
- M.C.
- Thurifer (Boat Bearer optional)
- Server 1 / Server 2
- Cross Bearer
- Book Bearer
- Candle Bearers (2)
- Torch Bearers (6, or 4 if the Candle Bearers are to double as Torch Bearers)

Pontifical Masses
- M.C.
- Thurifer / Boat Bearer
- Server 1 / Server 2
- Cross Bearer
- Book Bearer
- Candle Bearers (2)
- Torch Bearers (6, or 4 if the Candle Bearers are to double as Torch Bearers)
- Crozier Bearer / Miter Bearer

The Liturgy of the Hours

Vespers
- M.C.
- Cross Bearer
- Candle Bearers (2)
- Thurifer (Boat Bearer optional)
- Book Bearer

If fewer altar servers are available, the Cross Bearer can double as the Thurifer. If needed, one or both of the Candle Bearers may be omitted if needed.

Tenebræ
- M.C.
- Book Bearer
- At least two servers are required to extinguish the candles on the hearse, though in a pinch the M.C. and Book Bearer can do double duty here.

Holy Week

Palm Sunday
- M.C.
- Aspergilium
- Thurifer (Boat Bearer optional)
- Server 1 / Server 2
- Cross Bearer
- Book Bearer
- Candle Bearers (2)
- Torch Bearers (6, or 4 if the Candle Bearers are to double as Torch Bearers)

Holy Thursday
- M.C. (an assistant M.C. can be helpful)
- Thurifer (Boat Bearer optional)
- Server 1 / Server 2
- Cross Bearer
- Book Bearer
- Candle Bearers (2)
- Torch Bearers (6, or 4 if the Candle Bearers are to double as Torch Bearers)
- Bell Ringers (for *Gloria*–other servers can double up for this duty)
- Servers to help with the Mandatum (Washing of the Feet) (other servers can double up for this duty)

If an outdoor procession to the altar of repose is contemplated, add the following:
- Second Thurifer
- Four Baldachin (canopy) Bearers (often the Knights of Columbus are happy to take up this duty)
- Torch Bearers will carry their torches in procession

Good Friday
- M.C.
- Server 1 / Server 2 (also Cross holders for the Adoration of the Cross)
- Book Bearer
- Candle Bearers (2 to walk beside Cross and take up their station beside it for Adoration)
- Candle Bearers (2 for Communion, also with purificators for the Adoration of the Cross)
- Torch Bearers (6)

The Easter Vigil
- M.C. (an assistant M.C. can be helpful)
- Thurifer (Boat Bearer optional)
- Server 1 (also responsible for incense grains / lighting altar candles during *Gloria* / recessional candles)
- Server 2 (Also responsible for lucifer during the Blessing of the Fire and the Preparation of the Candle / lighting altar candles during *Gloria* / recessional candles)
- Cross Bearer

- Server to hold Easter Candle during the Preparation of the Candle)
- Book Bearer (Missal)
- Book Bearer (Exsultet–may not be required, depending on your logistics)
- Candle Bearers (2 for Procession, Exsultet, Recessional)
- Aspergilium
- Bell Ringers (for *Gloria*–other servers can double up for this duty)
- Torch Bearers (6)

Eucharistic Processions

Presuming this will take place immediately following Mass, the normal servers for a solemn Mass are supplemented by:

- Second Thurifer
- Four Baldachin (canopy) Bearers (often the Knights of Columbus are happy to take up this duty)
- Six Torch Bearers will carry their torches in procession

Baptisms, Weddings, Funerals

If this will take place in the context of a Mass, the usual servers are required as for Mass, with the addition of an Aspergilium.

If no Mass is to be celebrated:

- Cross Bearer
- Candle Bearers (2)
- Book Bearer
- Aspergilium
- For funerals, add Thurifer (Boat Bearer optional)

Devotions

Benediction of the Blessed Sacrament
    Thurifer (Boat Bearer optional)
    M.C. (or additional server)
    Torch Bearers (an even number; optional)

Stations of the Cross
    Cross Bearer
    Torch (or Candle) Bearers (2)

		Thurifer / Boat Bearer	Crucifer / Book Bearer	Server 1 / Server 2	Candlebearer (and Torches for Eucharistic Prayer)	MC	TEAM
February 14, 2018 Ash Wednesday	7:15 AM	Mr. Rose	Preston W.	Francis C.	Junior P.	**Mr. Ryng**	
		Chandler W.	Benjamin B.	Noah B.	Danny P.		
February 16, 2018	7:00 PM		Noah C.	Max C.	Francis C.		Stations of the Cross
1st Sunday of Lent							
February 17, 2018 *Saturday Vigil*	5:00 PM		Wayne H.	**Mr. Ryng**		*(Mr. Ryng)*	V
			(Crucifer)	Abigaile H.			
February 18, 2018 *Sunday Mass*	Noon	Francis C.	Adam R.	Mark R.	Merick R.	**Mr. Ryng**	B
			(Crucifer)	Jasmine V.	Joseph V.		
Sunday Vespers	6:00 PM	Francis C.	Noah C.			Mr. Ryng	
February 23, 2018	4:00 PM	Monthly Altar Server Meeting - Server 1&2 and Thurifer (Re)training					Church
	7:00 PM		Mr. Ryng	Francis C.	Noah C.		Stations of the Cross
2nd Sunday of Lent							
February 24, 2018 *Saturday Vigil*	5:00 PM	Abigaile H.	Chandler W.	Preston W.		**Mr. Ryng**	V
			Claire H.	Wayne H.			
February 25, 2018 *Sunday*	Noon	Theresa R.	Noah C.	Francis C.	Max C.	**Mr. Rose**	A
			Angelo A.	Peter S.			
	6:00 PM	Mr. Rose	Abigaile H.		Wayne H.	Mr. Ryng	
		Theresa R.			Claire H.		Solemn Vespers
March 2, 2018	7:00 PM		Noah C.	Adam R.	Max C.		Stations of the Cross
3rd Sunday of Lent							
March 3, 2018 *Saturday Vigil*	5:00 PM		Wayne H.	**Mr. Ryng**		*(Mr. Ryng)*	V
			Claire H.	Abigaile H.			
March 4, 2018 *Sunday*	Noon	Theresa R.	Jasmine V.	Adam R.	Merick R.	**Mr. Rose**	B
			(Crucifer)	Mark R.	Joseph V.		
Scrutinies	6:00 PM	Theresa R.			Noah C.	Mr. Ryng	
					Francis C.		Solemn Vespers
March 9, 2018	7:00 PM		Abigaile H.	Wayne H.	Claire H.		Stations of the Cross
4th Sunday of Lent	(Laetare Sunday)						
March 10, 2018 *Saturday Vigil*	5:00 PM	Abigaile H.	Chandler W.	Abbie W.		**Mr. Ryng**	V
			Claire H.	Wayne H.			
March 11, 2018 *Sunday*	Noon	Angelo A.	Theresa R.	Noah C.	Peter S.	**Mr. Rose**	A
			(Crucifer)	Max C.	Francis C.		
Scrutinies	6:00 PM	Mr. Rose	Abigaile H.		Wayne H.	Mr. Ryng	
					Claire H.		Solemn Vespers
March 16, 2018	7:00 PM		Adam R.	Preston W.	Chandler W.		Stations of the Cross
5th Sunday of Lent							
March 17, 2018 *Saturday Vigil*	5:00 PM		Chandler W.	**Mr. Ryng**		*(Mr. Ryng)*	V
			(Crucifer)	Preston W.			
March 18, 2018 *Sunday*	Noon	Theresa R.	Merick R.	Mark R.		**Mr. Rose**	B
		Adam R.	Joseph V.	Jasmine V.			
Scrutinies	6:00 PM	Francis C.	Noah C.			Mr. Ryng	
							Solemn Vespers
March 23, 2018	7:00 PM		Abigaile H.	Wayne H.	Claire H.		Stations of the Cross

		Thurifer / Boat Bearer	Crucifer / Book Bearer	Server 1 / Server 2	Candlebearer (and Torches for Eucharistic Prayer)	MC	TEAM
HOLY WEEK							

HOLY WEEK

Palm Sunday

		Thurifer / Boat Bearer	Crucifer / Book Bearer	Server 1 / Server 2	Candlebearer (and Torches for Eucharistic Prayer)	MC	TEAM
March 24, 2018	9:00 AM	REHEARSAL	*Easter Vigil Rehearsal*				
	12:30 PM	REHEARSAL	*Palm Sunday Rehearsal*				
Saturday Vigil	5:00 PM	Mr. Rose	Theresa R.	Abigaile H.	Wayne H.	**Mr. Ryng**	V
			Abby W.	Preston W.	Claire H.	Asp: Abby W.	
		Torch Bearers:	(Wayne H.)	(Claire H.)			
March 25, 2018	Noon	Mr. Rose	Jasmin V.	Mark R.	Merrick R.	**Mr. Ryng**	A
Sunday		Adam R.	Theresa R.	Francis C.	Joseph V.	Asp: Noah C.	
		Torch Bearers:	(Merrick R.)	(Joseph V.)			
	6:00 PM	Mr. Rose	Noah C.		Theresa R.	**Mr. Ryng**	
			Abigaile H.		Francis C.		
					Wayne H.		
					Claire H.		**Solemn Vespers**
March 28, 2018	5:00 PM	REHEARSAL	*Good Friday Rehearsal*				
Wednesday	8:00 PM		Francis C.		Theresa R.	**Mr. Ryng**	
			Abigaile H.		Wayne H.	Mr. Rose	
					Noah C.		
					Claire H.		*Tenebrae*
March 29, 2018 *Thursday of the Lord's Supper*	7:00 PM			*At Visitation Church*			
March 30, 2018	9:00 AM	Mr. Rose	(Thurifer)		**Mr. Ryng**		*Lauds*
			(Mr. Ryng)		Theresa R.		
Good Friday	Noon			**Mr. Rose**	Theresa R.		*Tre Ore*
	3:00 PM		**Abigaile H.**	Wayne H.	Claire H.		*Stations of the Cross*
	7:00 PM	MC: **Mr. Ryng**		Mr. Rose	Abigaile H.	CB: **Junior P.**	
			Wayne H.	Noah C.	Francis C.	CB: **Danny P.**	
		Torch Bearers:	*Theresa R.*	Deke S.	Lenny S.	Claire H.	
March 31, 2018	9:00 AM	Mr. Rose	(Thurifer)		Abigaile H.		*Lauds*
		Theresa R.	**Mr. Ryng**		Wayne H.		
					Claire H.		
Holy Saturday **EASTER VIGIL**	1:00 PM	REHEARSAL	*Easter Vigil Rehearsal*				
	8:30 PM	Francis C.	Noah C.	Mark R.	HR: Theresa R.	MC: **Mr. Ryng**	
			BB: Benjamin B.	Noah B.	Vis: Jacob B.	MC2: Mr. Rose	
			Ex: Merrick R.	Asp: **Jacob B.**	Asp: **Noah C.**	MC3: Noah C.	
		Torch Bearers:	*Joshua B.*	Danny P.	Jacob B.		
			Theresa R.	Junior P.	Merrick R.		
		Recessional Candles	Theresa R.	Jacob B.			
		Bells:	Merrick R.	Mark R.			
April 1, 2018 **Easter Sunday**	Noon	Abigaile H.	Theresa R.	Adam R.	Joseph V.	Mr. Rose	
		Deke S.	Jasmin V.	Wayne H.	Claire H.		
		Torch Bearers:	Lenny S.	Claire H.			
			Joseph V.	Jasmin V.			

Additional servers always welcome. If you wish to serve, come to the Sacristy and speak with Mr. Ryng, Mr. Rose, or Father.

If you are unable to serve, you are responsible for finding your own replacement!

Apprentice Servers are encouraged to serve at all Masses they attend.

CROSS-REFERENCES TO ELLIOTT

Beauty, then, is not mere decoration, but rather an essential element of the liturgical action, since it is an attribute of God himself and His revelation. These considerations should make us realize the care which is needed, if the liturgical action is to reflect its innate splendour. — *Pope Benedict XVI*

BISHOP ELLIOTT'S BOOKS ON THE CELEBRATION of the modern Roman Rite are especially useful reference works in the planning and celebration of the sacred liturgy. In 2019, Ignatius Press published the third volume in this series, titled *Ceremonies Explained for Servers*. Since that book and this cover much of the same ground, albeit with a slightly different audience and emphasis, a cross-reference guide between that book and this might prove useful, at least where the various actions and movements of the servers are concerned.

Topics in Elliott	paragraphs	in this book
Ceremonial Actions	111–199	
Objects	112–130	"Sacred Books, Vessels, and Linens" on page 94
Vestments	131–151	"Sacred Vestments" on page 90
Server robes	152–153	"Vesture" on page 16, and "Altar Server Vesture" on page 133
Basic actions	154–191	"Common Ceremonial Actions" on page 18
Hands	160–162	throughout the section "Standing, Sitting, and Kneeling" on page 19
Sign of the Cross	163–173	"The Sign of the Cross" on page 22
Sitting	174–175	"Sitting" on page 20
Walking	176–177	"Walking" on page 21
Kneeling	178–179	"Kneeling" on page 20
Genuflections	180–188	"Genuflecting" on page 23
Bows	189–191	"Bowing" on page 26
Movement in the Sanctuary	192–199	"Walking" on page 21
Procedures during Mass	200–246	"Altar Server Duties" on page 55; see also specific sections below
Book	201–205	"" on page 31
Candles	206–209	"Candles" on page 30
Presentations	210–215	throughout "Altar Server Duties" on page 55
Washing the Priest's Hands	216–217	"Lavabo" on page 70 and (for a single server) "Lavabo" on page 80
Preparing the Chalice on the Altar	218–229	"Arranging the Altar" on page 34
Bells	230–231	"Ringing the Bells" on page 33
Thurible	232–244	"Incensing" on page 35
Carrying the Cross	245–246	"Processional Cross" on page 30

APPENDIX: FORMS

Altar Server Application Form

Name of Server:	

| **Date of Birth:** | **Sacraments Received:** | ☐ Baptism   ☐ Confirmation |
| | | ☐ 1st Holy Communion |

Parent(s) or Guardian(s) of Server:

Mailing Address:

Parent or Guardian Phone:

Parent or Guardian Email:

Preferred Mass:

☐ Saturday Vigil   ☐ Sunday 8AM   ☐ Sunday 10AM   ☐ Sunday 4PM

☐ Would ONLY be able to serve at the above Mass

☐ Would be able to serve at the following other Masses:

Time: _____   ☐ regularly   ☐ on occasion

Time: _____   ☐ regularly   ☐ on occasion

☐ Would like to be invited to serve at other parish liturgies:

☐ funerals   ☐ weddings   ☐ major feasts   ☐ vespers

Expectations of the Altar Server

1. Must have received their first Holy Communion.
2. Must have parents or other parishioners who agree to support their ministry and bring them **30 minutes early** to Mass on the days when they are serving.
3. Must adhere to dress code.
4. Must be willing and able to come to trainings and rehearsals.

Please place your completed form in the collection basket.

Name:

Training Level:

Last Assessment:

	Date	Served As	Signature	Notes
1				
2				
3				
4				
5				
6				
7				
8				
9				
10				
11				
12				
13				
14				
15				
16				
17				
18				
19				
20				
21				
22				
23				
24				
25				